A Book of Rock & Roll Quotes
Mouthing Off

John D. Luerssen

Photos by Rahav Segev, Jason Homa,
and Dominic Episcopo

THE TELEGRAPH COMPANY
BROOKLYN, NEW YORK
PITTSBURGH, PENNSYLVANIA

Cover collage concept by Adam Beating
Layout by Dan Shepelavy
Photographs © 2002 Rahav Segev, Jason Homa, Dominic Episcopo

LCCN 2001099802

A light bulb went off in my head one Wednesday evening in early 2000, when I was talking with Alex Chilton by phone for a *Rolling Stone* Q&A article. Alex, the brainchild behind influential '70s act Big Star, was promoting his latest solo album, *Set,* but he was telling me the story of his early rise to fame.

"I've been performing in the public eye since I was sixteen," the Memphis-born Chilton said with his lazy Southern inflection. "In fact, at the time I was failing the tenth grade and I was going to have to repeat my sophomore year in high school, but I got lucky and had a No. 1 hit that summer. So my mom and dad were like, "Why don't you go ahead and give this 'rock' thing a try?"

As Chilton spoke of his Box Tops hit "The Letter," I thought, "that's a great quote," prompting the hamster on the wheel in my mind to start moving. Once the concept was hatched, I set about the arduous task of gathering and organizing the material that would eventually materialize here. I could go on and on about the months spent compiling this material in my basement office, but you'd be bored, and after eighteen months of research, my fingers are getting tired of typing.

So here they are, the often obnoxious, sometimes introspective and remarkably honest musings of our globe's most cherished and acclaimed rock & roll personalities. Culled together for your entertainment, I'm calling it *Mouthing Off,* because – as any rock scribe will tell you – that's what rockers do best.

Cheers!

John D. Luerssen
January 2002

For Heidi, Meredith and Hayley

"Contents"

Bjork

Photo by Rahav Segev/Photopass.com

"No matter how posh a hotel you put me in, I'm still going to be this drunken slob at the end of it."
  – *Norman Cook* a.k.a. **Fatboy Slim** (2001)

"The Replacements gave me a new respect for drinking. They took drinking a lot to this new art form level – not about being a total idiot, but about being this beautifully perfect drunk."
  – *Billie Joe Armstrong* of **Green Day** (1996)

"I don't understand beer, it's like drinking wood."
  – *Bjork* (1996)

"It's way better to play and record with a few beers. Your hand settles down and you're not sweating, and it makes for better performances."
  – *Bob Pollard* of **Guided By Voices** (2001)

"There's nothing like throwing up out a bus door, going 65 miles an hour."
  – *Izzy Stradlin* of **Guns N' Roses** (1989)

"What's the point of going to college if you can't drink beer?"
  – *Josh Homme* of **Queens Of The Stone Age** (2000)

"I can honestly say, all the bad things that ever happened to me were directly attributed to drugs and alcohol. I mean, I would never urinate at the Alamo at nine o'clock in the morning dressed in a woman's evening dress sober."
  – *Ozzy Osbourne* (1992)

"I'm trying hard to become an alcoholic to fit into this whole rock & roll scene. I'm learning how to drink beer. I think I like Corona a little bit. I try really hard."
  – *Gwen Stefani* of **No Doubt** (1996)

"I'm a drunk, but I'm not a bad drunk. Well, maybe I'm the worst kind of drunk because I don't wake up in the morning and think, 'Oh my God, I can't believe I did that.'"
– *Chris Cornell* of **Soundgarden** (1996)

"Most people don't understand getting loaded. They understand 'recreational drinking.' Drinking to me is like getting on the Internet; it makes it easier to communicate with more people and have fun doing it. When I get a little tipsy, it's like 56K, and when I'm fucked up, it's like DSL. You forget about things, and I've got a lot of ugly shit to forget about."
– *Ian Sefchick* of **Creeper Lagoon** (2001)

"A lot of whatever you call alternative rock just waters down the same shit that fucking Blue Cheer and the Byrds were doing 25 years ago."
  — *Page Hamilton* of **Helmet** (1994)

"Whatever was sincere about the whole back-to-basics college rock thing that eventually turned into grunge — the whole 'We're not pretentious rock icons, we're normal people playing earnestly' — is over."
  — *Trent Reznor* of **Nine Inch Nails** (1995)

"There was the girl band thing, there was the foxcore farce, there was the Seattle band farce, there was the grunge rock thing. We've been around longer than all that stuff. Basically, we're a rock band from Los Angeles."
  — *Donita Sparks* of **L7** (1994)

"It's really sad that rock, especially alternative rock, has become corporate business."
  — *Billy Corgan* of **Smashing Pumpkins** (1995)

"The marketplace has turned around for better or worse. You go through your whole life saying, 'This is me,' and you're not into trends or fashion. And the next thing you know, what you do is perceived as trendy or fashionable. It's really strange."
  — *Kim Thayill* of **Soundgarden** (1994)

"I think that what people are classifying as alternative is nothing more than popular music. The tag 'alternative' confuses me. I can't make sense of it anymore; because it's not the alternative it's the staple. Rock with shorts on is alternative."
  — *Perry Farrell* of **Jane's Addiction** (1996)

"All the bands that wanted to be Guns N' Roses or U2 want to be Nirvana. As soon as someone says, 'Okay, alternative rock is big and that's the thing that makes money now,' then it eats itself alive."
  — *Flea* of **The Red Hot Chili Peppers** (1992)

"I have this theory about alternative rock. You have to have one guy in the band that sucks. If you don't, you just become prog-rock. Take Nirvana, Dave and Chris are both amazing players, but Kurt sucked as a guitarist. In the Posies, I suck, so that's the difference between us and a band like Rush."

— *Ken Stringfellow* of **The Posies** (1996)

"When we got signed, the floodgates were open. If you didn't get signed then, you probably weren't in a band. By the time we got the Warner Brothers backing behind us, we were aware that you had to sell records. You can't just make them and spend all your advances on drugs."

— *Wayne Coyne* of **The Flaming Lips** (1999)

"For a start, I've got to be out of my head to write."
   – *Shane MacGowan* of **The Pogues** (1989)

"Most of the lyrics are half remembered dreams, written down on scraps of toilet paper – dialogue I probably should have spoken to someone years ago, but I didn't have the guts to do it."
   – *Jonathan Donahue* of **Mercury Rev** (1998)

"I never wanted to sing. I just wanted to play rhythm guitar in the back and just play. But during the high school years, when I was playing guitar in my bedroom, I at least had the intuition that I had to write my own songs."
   – *Kurt Cobain* of **Nirvana** (1994)

"People think it's glamorous, songwriting, but this is what it's really about, walking around singing to yourself like a loony."
   – *Elvis Costello* (1995)

"My songs are my kids and some of them stay with me. Some others I have to send out, out to the war. It might sound stupid and it might even sound naïve, but that's just the way it is."
   – *Thom Yorke* of **Radiohead** (2000)

"Writing is always just the most fun imaginable. And also unspeakable. I do try to avoid it. That's why I have deadlines."
   – *Lou Reed* (2000)

"My idea is to write the Thriller of modern rock, have eight hit songs on it. Eight hit songs. Then everyone will be kissing my ass."
   – *Ben Folds* (2001)

"I could write a cutesy song, but I'd have to make it sick – 'On a nice summer's day I met a cute bunny rabbit. And buttfucked it.'"
   – *Jonathan Davis* of **Korn** (1998)

"Whenever I write lyrics I live through them. In a way they reflect a certain period in my life and I live through that period of my life again – relive the whole thing and that's pretty hard. I want to say what I feel and what I think, maybe because there are not a lot of female artists who voice what I feel."
  – *Gwen Stefani* of **No Doubt** (2000)

"It's a physical, emotional, and intellectual process. Not to sound too high falutin' about it, but it's an immediate process that involves all my faculties. It's an interplay between the conscious and subconscious."
  – *Moby* (2000)

"I think my foremost problem was that it got to be very important to write heavy songs. I mean, I never thought they were heavy when I wrote them, but gradually I got the impression they were by the way people related to them."
  – *Jackson Browne* (1996)

"Our songs collapse and grow and learn like children. People adopt them and learn to love them. They take care of them and defend them against people with black souls."
  – *Ian Sefchick* of **Creeper Lagoon** (2001)

"I write a song because I am deeply moved to write a song. It's a very simple process in that way."
  – *Adam Duritz* of **Counting Crows** (1996)

"There's no real logic to it. I may do two rock & roll albums in a row at some point, or I may do two soft ones in a row, or I may do some different kind of album that everybody wonders what the hell I did that for. I mean, I could do that. You know, it just depends, and there's no plan. I'm just going with the songs. The songs dictate the direction."
  – *Neil Young* (2000)

"It's easier to write about things that are falling apart than things that are beautiful and perfect. That's the nature of creation – as soon as

something is perfected and realized, it's immediately decaying. That's the first rule of the universe."
     – *Beck* (1996)

"Our songwriting and the way we sound really sucks."
     – *Paul Leary* of **Butthole Surfers** (1993)

"I'm really wary of anyone who discusses their writing with me or tells me they wrote about this or that. That should be apparent when I hear the song, rather than them trying to help me out."
     – *Tom Petty* (1996)

"Writing does come a lot from a place of sadness. It's sadness relief on a certain level. Expressing it through music gives you hope, and I guess that's what art is – kind of finding hope in the horror that life is and rendering it somehow."
     – *Matthew Sweet* (2001)

"It's actually really hard to write a happy song without sounding corny."
     – *Elliott Smith* (2001)

"Writing for me is like mental housecleaning."
     – *Carl Bell* of **Fuel** (2000)

"I've always wanted to write things that everybody could relate to. It was never that important to me to be beloved by hipsters."
     – *Dan Wilson* of **Semisonic** (2001)

"If I wrote the songs that the world wanted me to do, I would have been making 'All Day And All Of The Night' for the next twenty years."
     – *Ray Davies* of **The Kinks** (1998)

"Songwriting is a solitary life. And I don't have the self-discipline to stick at it. If you call me up and say, 'It's a lovely day, man - let's get the

bikes out and have a blast,' I'll say, 'All right.' I don't say, 'I can't come out, I've got to write a song.' I've never said that to anybody."
   – *Mark Knopfler* of **Dire Straits** (2000)

"I'm definitely into that line between obsessive and sane. I like taking normal, romantic 'love song' lyrics and putting the worst of overtones to it."
   – *Scott McCloud* of **Girls Against Boys** (1996)

"A lot of times I come up with a title that's so cool I have to write a song for it."
   – *Bob Pollard* of **Guided By Voices** (1996)

"To me, songwriting is almost like stamp collecting – except that I collect fragments of other people's lives."
   – *David Gedge* of **The Wedding Present** (1993)

"When people put records out, there is no way they are gonna know what the audience is going to think. If they sit around and wonder, 'What kind of song should I write? What am I trying to get people to feel?' They're just projecting their own feeling onto the people they think they're making records for."
   – *Hope Sandoval* of **Mazzy Star** (1996)

"Laboring over a three minute song is not my idea of a good time."
   – *Reverend Horton Heat* (1994)

"Our songs never come out the way we envision them. We surprise ourselves all the time because every time someone comes in to add a different layer it changes the sound around. By the end, you don't even know where the beginning was."
   – *David Baker* of **Mercury Rev** (circa 1993)

"I write lyrics after the music. I've always thought in pictures and images. So I never write anything down unless I have to. I'll listen to the music and get a series of images in my head and describe what I see in a story. It doesn't always come from music; it can come from

memories or what's going on in the world. But I don't think of music and lyrics as equal. To me, lyrics are only about one-fifth of the whole thing."
    – *Bernard Sumner* of **New Order** (1993)

"We're really prolific. If we're in a room together we can write song after song at will. Daniel Johnston's a slacker compared to us."
    – *Russell Simmins* of **The Jon Spencer Blues Explosion** (1996)

"Midnight Oil isn't a means of promulgating an ideology or a set of beliefs or principles or anything else for that matter. It's just not. It's just about songs. The songs come out and then if there's a political message in them, well so be it."
    – *Peter Garrett* of **Midnight Oil** (1993)

"The way I write, it encapsulates that moment or that day I wrote it and what I was thinking about. I forever have to relive that every time I sing about it. I'm not looking forward to going out there and playing "Unsatisfied" anymore, because I can't give that true credence. When you've got a head full of blow, and you've been up for three nights and you don't know where you are, and you don't know where you're going, that song hits home in a serious ugly way."
    – *Paul Westerberg*, ex-**The Replacements** (1993)

"I'm not trying to produce anything that makes people go, 'Oh wow, that was clever.' A lot of the old songs have words as foliage, verbiage, a screen of words. There was a big gap between expression and communication. But I've got more confidence about my songs now. I wanted to get something that has feeling in it. That's close, kind of right in your third eye."
    – *Robyn Hitchcock* (1993)

"I think that we're trying to write songs. There's more going on than a couple of distortion pedals and cranking it up and making some noise."
    – *John Curley* of **The Afghan Whigs** (1998)

"I know the process is to write a lot of shitty songs before the good ones start coming."
  – *Mary Lou Lord* (1995)

"I tried to write these meaningful songs and always, the whole time, I would come back to monkeys and chickens and frogs."
  – *Chris Ballew* of **The Presidents of The United States** (1995)

"The germination of a song, it's core, comes from the inside and thinking how to make a song that fills some kind of need at this time. But then with knowing that I try to pull in as much from the outside as possible, so that more people can listen to the music and have an in."
  – *Will Oldham* of **Palace Music** (2001)

"Even if I were talentless, after seeing Echo and The Bunnymen eight million times and Nirvana ten million times, how could I not write an okay new wave record?"
  – *Courtney Love* of **Hole** (1994)

"Some of my songs are positive and stuff, but some are about staring down at the ground and obsessing about stupid shit and being really teenage about it."
  – *Lou Barlow* of **Sebadoh** (1997)

"I don't think my music's weird. I just improvise and use the first thing that comes to mind. If I spend a couple weeks writing something, it lacks life. It doesn't have any of the needed mistakes."
  – *Beck* (1996)

"I write about boys, TV, and sleep disorders."
  – *Anna Waronker* of **That Dog** (1995)

"The songs don't give a fuck what I'm thinking about. They just play, and I hear them and I record them as honestly as I can. So I often don't know what I'm singing about, and that's where the dreamlike

quality comes from. A song, I believe, is a real thing. It has heat and electricity and energy and a voice. A song just doesn't wear outfits. And yet they use words in a very emotional, very active way, the way dreams use images. So they don't make linear sense."
   – *Kristin Hersh* of **Throwing Muses** (1994)

"I dread writing lyrics. I don't know who to get mad at that I have to do it. I write them after the music. I'm starting to feel compelled to jot things down now. I'm so unorganized. I generally don't have a cassette deck, or even a pen, so I say, 'Oh fuck it,' and it's gone."
   – *Jeff Martin* of **Idaho** (circa 1995)

"When I'm writing my songs, I get to parts of me I've hidden for so long. And it's a liberating place to be."
   – *Tori Amos* (1996)

"I trained myself to write on the spot. Anybody can do it, too, if they're willing to let go of worrying about failure and embarrassment in front of people."
   – *Jack Logan* (1994)

"Songs should live in the listener's mind. The great thing is when there is more to it than meets the eye. With a lot of didactic stuff you know what the song's about, you know what it's for, everything's explained, and everything is over in three minutes. There's no ambiguity, no confusion. There's no chance to savor the song over and over."
   – *Robyn Hitchcock* (1993)

"I like the way my lyrics are. Okay, they're a bit different but maybe that's the reason I like them. It's okay if people don't like the lyrics. Everybody should have their own opinion about them."
   – *Chino Moreno* of **The Deftones** (2000)

"I could write gloomy songs all day long, but I just don't see the point."
   – *Robert Smith* of **The Cure** (1992)

"After all these years of pop music, why are there so many girl songs? What else is there to write about?"
    – *Rivers Cuomo* of **Weezer** (2001)

"Sometimes you don't care about trying to make the lyrics make sense. Fuck, it's only lyrics."
    – *Noel Gallagher* of **Oasis** (1996)

"Stealing people's music is a good way to start writing a song."
    – *Justine Frischmann* of **Elastica** (1995)

"I write ideas down 24-hours a day. Even if I dream something cool, I force myself to get out of bed and write it down. Then I take my favorite poems and write melodies to them."
    – *Bob Pollard* of **Guided By Voices** (2001)

"My songs are just little letters to me."
    – *Fiona Apple* (1999)

"In rock music, most people adopt this narrative style they learned in the sixth grade. You know, What-I-Did-On-My-Summer-Vacation essay style. I feel like I write lyrics closer to the way people speak in real life."
    – *David Lowery* of **Cracker** (1994)

"Fear is my constant companion. How many melodies are there left in the world? But I've forced myself to embrace that fear. I have no choice. I'm a professional songwriter and member of a band."
    – *Pat DiNizio* of **The Smithereens** (1994)

"Rebellion, love, hate, sex, denial: all these will still be here when we're done. I like to stick to the old standbys in my songs."
    – *Paul Westerberg*, ex-**The Replacements** (1993)

"I don't exactly know where all the lyrics come from, but I trust myself implicitly, that there is a reason for them."
    – *Steven Kilbey* of **The Church** (1994)

"I write albums for myself and I try to make it something I would listen to. I operate under the idea that I'm not unusual. And if I try to do it really well for myself, other people can relate to it, too. But I don't really know how to write for other people so I can't do that."
   — *Lou Reed* (1998)

"We basically harnessed the time-tested Duke Ellington principle: feels good is good. And we would write a song real fast. We'd play it. We'd bash it out a few times, and if everyone's coats were glossy, and their tails were wagging, I reckoned that was good enough. You know, I said, 'Was that fun or what?' And it was like, 'Fuck yeah.' And I'd go, 'Good, then it was a song.'"
   — *Henry Rollins,* ex-**Black Flag** (2000)

"To be honest, we don't really know what it is we're doing. We're never sure how things will turn out. Each song is a small victory… Our music reflects an attitude of uncompromising strength, yet, at the same time, a fragile sense of uncertainty."
   — *Kevin Shields* of **My Bloody Valentine** (1991)

"We don't sing about Satan. We don't sing about sex and murder and skulls. My lyrics are purposely ambiguous so people have to think about what the fuck I'm talking about."
   — *Al Jourgensen* of **Ministry** (1999)

"We knew we needed a 'chant' song, because the Bay City Rollers had 'Saturday Night.'"
   — *Johnny Ramone,* discussing the origins of
      "Blitzkrieg Bop" (2001)

"'Rebel, Rebel' is just for me the funniest song. I can't, I just can't conceive how I wrote that now. I mean, I really must have felt that at the time but… Hot tramp, I love you so, don't give me grief. I mean it's really — it's so flippant."
   — *David Bowie* (1997)

"I truly believe this: there's songs that are written in five minutes and there's songs that are written in six months, and there's really nothing in the middle."
   – *David Lowery* of **Cracker** (1996)

"It's a little gross to put yourself in every song. I mean, how interesting do people really think you are?"
   – *Jakob Dylan* of **The Wallflowers** (2000)

"It's hard work, saving rock."
    – *The Edge* of **U2** (2000)

"At our very worst, we were better than most people. And at our very best, we could just wipe the floor with the lot of them."
    – *John Paul Jones* of **Led Zeppelin** (2001)

"Big bastards, that's what the Beatles were. You have to be a bastard to make it. And the Beatles were the biggest bastards on earth."
    – *John Lennon* (1980)

"We knew the band was good. I knew that every time I walked onstage. When no one spoke to each other – me and Joey basically didn't speak for a long time – I would still get up there every day, look at Joey, start to play and know, 'Yeah, I'm still in the best band in the world.'"
    –*Johnny Ramone* (2001)

"We're the most important group in the world, because we've got the best songs and we haven't even begun to show our potential yet."
    – *Ian Brown* of **The Stone Roses** (1990)

"You know, opening for Pearl Jam is the death slot."
    – *Stone Gossard* (1998)

"I can do things with a guitar that Eric Clapton probably hasn't even had a fucking nightmare about. Our instincts are worth more than a thousand years of guitar lessons."
    – *Jim Reid* of **The Jesus and Mary Chain** (1992)

"I know we're the best group in the world."
    – *Ian McCulloch* of **Echo & The Bunnymen** (circa 1984)

"We kind of tried to create a band that we would want to go and see. The only difference is that I'm the guitar player that you want to fuck now."
    – *Ruyter Suys* of **Nashville Pussy** (2000)

"God sent me to piss off the world."
   – *Eminem* (2000)

"We're the McDonald's of rock. We're always there to satisfy, and a billion served."
   – *Paul Stanley* of **Kiss** (1978)

"The fact of the matter is, I'm fucking brilliant. Not 'was' brilliant. 'Am' brilliant."
   – *Pete Townshend* (2000)

"I'm an artist and that means I can be as egotistical as I want to be."
   – *Lou Reed* (1998)

"We're like a fuckin' grenade and it's like everybody's struggling to hold the pin in!"
  – *Slash* of **Guns N' Roses** (1988)

"We used to joke about incorporating as a religion."
  – *Bob Weir* of **The Grateful Dead** (2001)

"If something is wrong with my band, I change it. If I feel someone's not enthusiastic in my band, I change it immediately. If you're in a band and you love rock, you've got to appreciate the opportunity that's been afforded you to quit your job and be in that band. There have been times where I can tell people in my band are not into it; it's too hard being on the road. OK, then, go back to working your day job."
  – *Bob Pollard* of **Guided By Voices** (2001)

"None of us gets exactly what we want, and you learn to live with that. It's something that I would never have believed I'd be able to do when I was twenty-four. I used to be like, 'Goddamnit, this is my song. I don't like that verse. Either you change it or I will.' Now it's like, 'Yeah. That's interesting.'"
  – *Peter Buck* of **R.E.M.** (1991)

"You have to find common ground because, of course, we don't respond to everything the same way. Josh doesn't have a problem going, 'Dude, I don't dig that riff.' We can disagree with each other without disrespecting each other. Sometimes when you argue you get all male, and when you get all fucking male, it becomes so much bigger than the verse of a song. Creative tension can be great for the music, but you can't let it overwhelm what you're doing."
  – *Keith Nelson* of **Buckcherry** (2001)

To be in a band, especially in a successful band means to deal with your doubts on a daily basis. It can be pretty hard and merciless."
  – *Gavin Rossdale* of **Bush** (1999)

"Bad Religion has always been a band of scathing social commentary, and that can be perceived as negative. We're all in our 30s now and we're not as angry as we were when we were 15 years old."
   – *Brian Baker* of **Bad Religion** (2000)

"We were supposed to be the alt-country Nirvana. I guess I was supposed to hang myself with a banjo string."
   – *Ryan Adams* of **Whiskeytown** (2000)

"I never sat down and said, 'Right. I want to be a singer.' I was a singer because Ian [Curtis] died."
   – *Bernard Sumner* of **New Order**, ex-**Joy Division** (1993)

"It's really a dysfunctional band."
   – *D'Arcy* of **Smashing Pumpkins** (1993)

"I don't see how a dysfunctional band could release 80 songs in five years."
   – *Billy Corgan* of **Smashing Pumpkins** (1997)

"Our band is a benevolent dictatorship. I welcome your opinion, but that doesn't mean it's an equal vote."
   – *Jon Bon Jovi* of **Bon Jovi** (2000)

"We know what it's like not to sell records and not have people love you, and that's okay with us."
   – *Vudi* of **American Music Club** (1994)

"It's just such cool chemistry between us. We've been together for so long and care about each other so much, it's really like brothers."
   – *Adam Yauch* of **Beastie Boys** (1998)

"We've always been our own breed of band. We concocted a unique sound and style all our own, a trademark. That's what everybody tries to achieve but so few really do."
   – *Joey Ramone* (1993)

"The government doesn't want you to have a good time, and sometimes your parents don't want you to have a good time. Guess what, baby? The Black Crowes want you to have a motherfucking good time."
   – *Chris Robinson* of **The Black Crowes**(1991)

"We don't want to be praised and idolized. We want our songs to be well regarded. Love our songs, don't love us."
   – *Andy Partridge* of **XTC** (1992)

"One of the great things about being in a band with other girls is you just don't come across the male ego trips."
   – *Justine Frischmann* of **Elastica** (1995)

"The band is really like family. And there's nothing from the outside world, or the inside, that could break us up."
   – *Ed Kowalcyzk* of **Live** (2001)

"When I was a Beatle, I thought we were the best fucking group in the world, and believing that is what made us what we were."
   – *John Lennon* (1980)

"We finally had to make a rule that nobody touches anyone onstage. And if you do, it's a fight."
   – *Mark Lanegan* of **The Screaming Trees** (1993)

"We want to stay an awkward, difficult, improvising band that some nights flies and some nights falls flat on its face."
   – *Tim Booth* of **James** (1994)

"We're a totally collaborative, psychotic, dysfunctional unit – just like any band."
   – *Butch Vig* of **Garbage** (1998)

"It's not easy to be in a group. It's like marriage without sex. The only lubricant you have is the music."
    – *Sting,* on being in **The Police** (circa 1983)

"We're not a fashionable band. In fact we look like shit."
    – *Les Claypool* of **Primus** (1993)

"When we're old and grey, we'll be able to sit around and tell our grandchildren we used to be a punk rock band touring the country in a van."
    – *Trever Keith* of **Face To Face** (1995)

"Rather than sit around and try to think about what our audience might be into, or any of that kind of crap, we just do stuff we get stoked about. By continuing to do that, it seems that we're being true to ourselves and people who like our bands can appreciate that."
    – *Bill Stevenson* of **All** and **The Descendents** (2000)

"I guess I'm not the biggest Replacements fan. I played some of our early records the other day, and the playing and singing – some of it was just atrocious! Still, being in a band with those particular guys was a very special thing. I knew it then, and I know it now."
    – *Paul Westerberg,* ex-**The Replacements** (1996)

"We're probably the first band to have a full-time, full-paid psychiatrist on the road."
    – *Dave Gahan* of **Depeche Mode** (1995)

"Most governments don't last as long as this band. It's a total democracy, with all the good things and bad things about being in democracy. Nobody's the leader, which is good, but that means nobody leads, which is bad. It's like a Ouija board, we are whatever we put our hands to each day."
    – *Peter Buck* of **R.E.M.** (1998)

"A record company is like a giant ATM machine."
   – *Beck* (1994)

"I want to sell records. I'd like to be more than just a jewel in my record label's crown. Somewhere between Van Morrison and Hootie and the Blowfish would be nice."
   – *Paul Westerberg,* ex-**The Replacements** (1996)

"I feel some pressure to have a hit. It's an occupational hazard."
   – *Shawn Colvin* (2001)

"I really don't like singles. Record companies don't really care for the artistic part of an album. They want a collection of hit singles to make sure the album sells. I'm not interested in it."
   – *Robert Smith* of **The Cure** (2000)

"There are guys that have had Top Ten hits that are fry cooks right now. They're in prison, or they're digging ditches, or they're living with their mom somewhere. It happens. You don't ever want to get overly confident in this business."
   – *Mike Mills* of **R.E.M.** (1991)

"Censorship sucks! It's just reality that we have to make edited versions so certain stores can sell our records."
   – *Joshua Todd* of **Buckcherry** (2000)

"We were one of the first underground bands to get signed, before Nirvana or Pearl Jam. It was like an experiment. Atlantic didn't know what to do with the group, so they pumped in a lot of money and the record obviously didn't meet their expectations. It didn't sell up against the Zeppelin catalog."
   – *Jeff McDonald* of **Redd Kross** (1994)

"We don't claim to be the only band to ever get fucked over by a major label."
   – *Britt Daniel* of **Spoon** (2001)

"I suppose if I was selling records like Matchbox Twenty or something, I would experience the same luxuries I get when I work on a Cameron Crowe movie. But I'm just playing in a small band, and in comparison the treatment you get from the movie business is unbelievable."
 – *Mark Kozelek* of the **Red House Painters** (2000)

"I have this feeling record companies used to have more music lovers working for them. Rather than all bankers the way it is now – mostly bankers."
 – *Evan Dando* of **The Lemonheads** (1996)

"I'd sell one of my songs for any commercial in the world that paid enough money."
 – *Scott Weiland* of **Stone Temple Pilots** (2001)

"I was in the mall and they had Crass T-shirts. Crass didn't make those! It seems like resistance is futile. It's hard to come to terms with that if you disagree with corporate capitalism. If you play music, eventually you deal with that."
 – *Sam Coomes* of **Quasi** (1999)

"I wish MTV didn't exist. I make music, I wish it was just you and the record."
 – *Lenny Kravitz* (1996)

"[MTV is] twenty-four hour access to a load of idiots with too much money and not enough sense.'
 – *Elvis Costello* (1983)

"When I see MTV, I wanna say, 'Fuck rock & roll. Rock & roll is dead. Art rules.'"
 – *Thurston Moore* of **Sonic Youth** (1994)

"Mark Eitzel told us, 'I saw the video for 'Jeremy,' and I fucking hated it.' It was so shocking, this guy we'd just met. He said, 'I had a totally

different vision of it, and that fucked up the whole thing.' And I agreed with him."
   — *Jeff Ament* of **Pearl Jam** (2001)

"MTV is pathetic. We have no place on it... I would almost rather say I don't want to be on the fuckin' thing."
   — *Billie Armstrong* of **Green Day** (1995)

"MTV is like, 'make us a video, make sure it's hot, spend a lot of money on it, and maybe we'll play it. And then we'll take the credit for it and play it as much as we want whenever we want.'"
   — *Stephen Malkmus* of **Pavement** (1994)

"Whenever you can buy hamburgers to your favorite songs, you know it's over."
   — *Peter Buck* of **R.E.M.** (circa 1996)

"There's a theory that, no matter how big these record companies get, they can really only work one record at a time. So, if Matchbox Twenty has something going on that week, you're fucked."
   — *Adam Schlesinger* of **Fountains of Wayne** (2001)

"A major label is your best friend when you're on the heatseeker chart, but if you put out an album that does nothing commercially, then they can't put enough distance between you."
   — *John Davis* of **Superdrag**, (2001)

"I know some people might think that Elektra is an odd label for us, but they never question the music. They know they'll sell a certain amount of our records in spread-out pockets around America. We've never had a big hit, but we make a good living out of something we love doing, which is our definition of success.
   — *Tim Gane* of **Stereolab** (1999)

"When I stop long enough to think about it, I can't believe that I could complain about selling only 100,000 records. I think of all the great bands like Big Star who never sold anywhere near that and I feel like an ingrate."
  — *Mike Connell* of **The Connells** (1993)

"It's easy to slip through a major label's hands, even when intentions at the outset are very good. A lot of political things go on."
  — *Tommy Keene* (1993)

"I've seen Behind The Music long enough to know how things work. But we don't worry about it too much. It's gonna suck no matter what, because artists basically get fucked unless you're, like, Madonna."
  — *Ben Benjamin* of **The Benjamins** (2001)

"Instead of giving Aerosmith $80 million, why not give forty bands $2 million? We don't need to hear Aerosmith again — already heard it."
  — *Mojo Nixon* (1997)

"If you look at the radio playlists of virtually every commercial station, modern rock, alternative or whatever, there's practically no independent music at all. They don't just say, "Hey this is cool, we'll play this." It's a political, calculated thing. It all comes down to label support, and most independent labels don't have the kind of backing it takes to break a record in that environment."
  — *Warren Fitzgerald* of **The Vandals** (2000)

"Promoting pop music ain't about nothing but whores and blow."
  — *Steve Earle* (2000)

"I've worked with inept A&R people in the past, and I'm sure with my luck I may in the future. Anyone who isn't an artist and works in this business and views it as a job, those tend to be the most frustrating people for me. At the end of the day, regardless of what happens, they get to go home, but I'm still in this band 24-7, and it's my life's work to make it successful."
  — *Trever Keith* of **Face To Face** (2000)

"You never know what the people at the record company are plotting, you know, either for or against you."
   – *John Curley* of **The Afghan Whigs** (1998)

"I remember the A&R men at CBS telling us that "Dog Eat Dog" and "Antmusic" were too noisy, and asking us to remix the tracks. We took the tape home, didn't touch it, and then took it back to them a couple of days later. 'Yes, that's much better,' they said."
   – *Adam Ant* (1995)

"Our years in the business have managed to take a lot of fun out of things. It's still fun playing, but they made us miserable. Maybe it was naïve of us to think it was gonna be a little easier than this. Nobody did anything for us. We got treated like shit."
   – *Joey Ramone* (1996)

"Any schmuck who puts on a festival without good, free drinking water available at a thousand points around the site shouldn't be in business. It's a lesson to promoters: Do it properly or we're going to bust your ass."
   – *Joe Strummer,* commenting on Woodstock '99 (1999)

"It does seem rather odd to me, the idea of putting huge amounts of people together at an Air Force base – with a lot of concrete – in the middle of the summer."
   – *Mike D* of **Beastie Boys**, commenting
      on Woodstock '99 (1999)

"Is it just about cucumbers down the trousers? Or is it about genuine people trying to say something? Having R.E.M. in the Top Ten means something – it means a lot to guys like me who are trying to ride their beast on their own terms."
   – *Billy Bragg* (1991)

"I just don't trust [major labels] anymore. I also don't really want somebody telling me I'm going to be a star when I know for a fucking

fact that I'm not going to be – and I don't care to be."
   – *Ryan Adams* of **Whiskeytown** (2001)

"It's nice to get a little recognition. If you wanna continue to have access to the things that you need to play music, you have to have some measure of popularity or recognition on some level. So you have to be conscious of it. In a perfect world it wouldn't matter at all, but it's nice to get a pat on the back. You can't eat a pat on the back, but it's okay."
   – *Sam Coomes* of **Quasi** (2001)

It doesn't seem like you can sell a record in America if you're a British band unless it's got a little sticker saying, 'shaggable band of the year,' or 'extra hidden CD format.' I don't know why they don't just put hundred dollar bills in some of the records and have a little sticker saying, 'This might contain a hundred dollar bill.'
   – *Damon Albarn* of **Blur** (1997)

"When people smell that they can potentially make a lot of money, doors open. I don't necessarily think that's a bad thing."
   – *Perry Farrell* of **Jane's Addiction** (2001),
      Lollapalooza co-founder

"The entertainment industry and music is full of a lot of impostors. I see a lot of people willingly and unwillingly having idiosyncrasies in their lives magnified into freak elements simply to land the cover of magazines. Those people don't know how lucky they are that they have anyone to listen to their music because they have nothing to say."
   – *Bob Mould* , of **Sugar**, ex-**Husker Du**(1996)

"This one guy at Warner Brothers told us to stop making pretentious, faggy videos. I though I looked really suave and handsome."
   – *Flea* of **The Red Hot Chili Peppers** (1996)

"What pisses me off is when I've got seven or eight record company fat pig men sitting there telling me what to wear."
   – *Sinead O'Connor* (1997)

"I like the music business because as horrible an empire as it is and as tacky as it is, it's always in transition. They try to control things as much as they can, but they can't – as much as they race around after it. And I like watching that because it's a real microcosm of society. You can't really control it. The safest thing is just to be aware of what is going on."
   – *Thurston Moore* of **Sonic Youth** (circa 1995)

"The whole major label thing leaves a bad taste in my mouth. I don't think that all major labels are bad, just like I don't think all indie labels are good. It really depends on the individual, just like anything else."
   – *Dexter Holland* of **The Offspring** (1997)

"I don't have any delusions about our standing in the market. Our record companies love us when we're selling records, but they hate us when we're not."
   – *Robert Smith* of **The Cure** (1996)

"I believe in unashamedly using and abusing the music industry to finance my holidays and freedom. Record companies are crap anyway. They'll destroy you and spit you out and then put a record out to capitalize on your death if they can. They boss you around and make you tour until you're nearly dead. I'm not going to be told what to do by anybody."
   – *Jaz Coleman* of **Killing Joke** (1996)

"This is an insecure business. Obviously I do very well but I'm not secure, and I have to get there. I have to ensure that I have the freedom to work. I'm still nervous about somebody taking my right to record away; all of them getting together and going, 'Nah, we don't want you anymore.' That's always in the back of my mind."
   – *Iggy Pop* (1993)

"I listened to producers and record company people when I started out because I thought they knew what the fuck was going on – what a mistake! I've learned that I've gotta move on and do what satisfies me,

not some asshole at some record company with a title who thinks
they know what people want."
  – *Al Jourgensen* of **Ministry** (1995)

"We're intensely snotty, which means that we don't give a fuck about
the 'bidness end of music. Sell the records or not. Who cares? We just
make 'em."
  – *Cris Kirkwood* of the **Meat Puppets** (1994)

"The music business is very immoral. That's why I got involved in it.
With music, you're expected to behave in an immoral way."
  – *Jarvis Cocker* of **Pulp** (1995)

"People in the music business were getting taught a lesson. Some guy
who drives a BMW, who has, like, four pounds of Rolex watch hanging
off his arm, is being taught new science by some guy with greasy hair,
who's not impressed by money, okay? That's very healthy."
  – *Henry Rollins* (1994)

"All we won was freedom. Those asswipes got the money. It turns out
freedom is very expensive."
  – *John Squire* of **The Stone Roses** on litigation
    with former record label, Silvertone (1991)

"If you want to get taken advantage of in this business, there are
plenty of people who will do it."
  – *Rodney Bottum* of **Faith No More** (1993)

"If the Lollapalooza tour bus had gone over a bridge, the music
business would be about 15 percent better off."
  – *Steve Albini* of **Shellac** (1994)

"We're actually releasing the next album on eBay, 'cause we think we
can get a better royalty rate."
  – *Pat Wilson* of **Weezer** (2001)

"I was a bitch a lot of the time…like the snotty little sister. I spent most of last tour at the back of the bus with the door shut."
— *Natalie Merchant,* ex-**10,000 Maniacs** (1995)

"Would you ever return to having your mother wipe your asshole?"
— *Julian Cope,* when asked if he'd ever again perform with **Teardrop Explodes** (1999)

"After The Pogues, I never wanted to touch another instrument."
— *Shane MacGowan* (1995)

"In the final analysis, the thing that used to make me happy was making me miserable and so I just had to get out."
— *Johnny Marr,* on his decision to quit **The Smiths** (1987)

"If a family member needed a kidney transplant, sure."
—*Frank Black* on the possibility of a **Pixies** reunion (2001)

"It may sound bitter, but all we really did together was drink. Thinking about the band is thinking about someone you knew in high school who you got drunk with a lot. There's not a lot of attachment. You move on and make other friends and do new things."
— *Chris Mars,* ex-**Replacements** (1992)

"It's like a salmon swimming upstream to lay her eggs and dying: She knows she's not going to go back out to the Glapagos Islands, or wherever it is, and conceive another batch of eggs and swim back up to Nova Scotia. She's got one load of eggs and that's it."
— *Robyn Hitchcock,* discussing the 1981 break-up of **The Soft Boys** (2000)

"Rick Rubin thinks he knows what's best for everybody. He was the expendable motherfucker."
— *Adam Horovitz* of **Beastie Boys**, on his former producer (1994)

"It was a complete fuck up. I did him wrong, I stabbed him in the back."

> -*Joe Strummer,* formerly of **The Clash,** on sacking his songwriting partner/bandmate Mick Jones (1989)

"We fired the guy to save his life. We could not continue thinking, 'Hmmm, maybe he'll get better.' We were criticized for being intolerant and not helping Jimmy when he needed us most. Believe me, the guy couldn't have had any more chances. He used up all his chances plus five."

> – *Billy Corgan,* rationalizes firing **Smashing Pumpkins** drummer Jimmy Chamberlin (1996)

"With Dire Straits, it was so damn big. You're a part of a traveling circus. The lighting rig came from Star Trek. When we got to the point of carrying around our own stage, I decided I had had enough."

> – *Mark Knopfler* (2000)

"I wasn't appreciated and I wasn't liked. I wanted to ride on the bus with the guys, womanize and get high and confide in them. I wanted some friends."

> – *Perry Farrell,* on the original break-up of **Jane's Addiction** (1993)

"It's like any romantic relationship or any friendship where you meet somebody and you really connect – you really see eye to eye. It's totally magical. But when you start disagreeing it can be crushing because you think, 'Wait, you're supposed to be just like me, and you're supposed to see things the same way.'"

> – *Nina Gordon,* on why she left **Veruca Salt** (2000)

"The rumor is I fired him. Actually, we had to quit playing together. We were going to kill each other. It was a total Noel and Liam kind of thing."

> – *Ryan Adams* of **Whiskeytown,** on the blow-up between him and original member Phil Wandscher (2000)

"I like working with other people in team situations. That's why I like working with bands, although I don't particularly like working in a committee. That was one of the problems from Dark Side Of The Moon onwards."
– *Roger Waters,* ex-**Pink Floyd** (2000)

"We just drifted apart. Crumbled."
– *John Squire,* formerly of **The Stone Roses** (1998)

"I was onstage feeling really bored with it all. The band had become an income generator instead of something to make music with. So I quit. I fired the band. I still love the guys in the band, but we couldn't work any more."
– *Mark Eitzel,* formerly of **American Music Club** (1996)

"We were never good at communicating. Anything we tried to collaborate on – a video, a tour schedule – it just never really worked. I was just tired of doing the same thing over and over, different song progressions that were starting to sound the same. It's hard to teach an old dog new tricks. Or a 30-year-old male."
– *Stephen Malkmus,* ex-**Pavement** (2001)

Stephen Malkmus, ex-Pavement

Photo by Dominic Episcopo

"We weren't too ambitious when we started out. We just wanted to be the biggest thing that ever walked the planet."
   – *Steven Tyler* of **Aerosmith** (1993)

"When we started out, they said you'll never play Camden, New Jersey. It took us 10 years, but here we are."
   – *Mark Arm* of **Mudhoney** (1998)

"I don't know what our future is. I envisioned it at the beginning as being able to play CBGB on a Wednesday night. Anything after that is a dreamland."
   – *Thurston Moore* of **Sonic Youth** (1995)

"Everybody's going, 'Isn't it great what Jamiroquai has achieved?' Well, to me is nothing. This is just a good foundation for a band I want to last for 15 or 20 years. I'm not interested in just being today's pop star. I want a career, like Stevie Wonder or Sting or Queen."
   – *Jason Kay* of **Jamiroquai** (1997)

"We were writing songs for arenas back when we were playing in a garage."
   – *Ed Kowalcyzk* of **Live** (1995)

"I don't want people to fucking worship me. I want people to be inspired to do something cool, take something form one of our shows into their life and charge them. Charge them so they can fight the good fight."
   – *John Reis* of **Rocket From The Crypt** (1999)

"I thought Black Flag should be the biggest thing in the world. And I thought everyone should be subjected to us, whether they wanted it or not."
   – *Greg Ginn* of **Black Flag** (2001)

"We want to be phalluses ramming in the butthole of pop."
   – *Gibby Haynes* of **The Butthole Surfers** (1993)

"When everyone else was throwing beer glasses at the stage and putting safety pins through their noses, all we wanted to do was eat cucumber sandwiches."
 – *Robyn Hitchcock,* on his days with **The Soft Boys** (2001)

"I'm just trying to make music that I'd like to hear right now, with the stupid faith that ultimately there must be other people like me."
 – *David Lowery* of **Cracker** (1996)

"Growing up, I so wanted to get the fuck out of where I was, away from the mediocrity and mundane-ness of rural life. Anything extreme caught my attention."
 – *Trent Reznor* of **Nine Inch Nails** (1994)

"I knew I didn't want to stick around my hometown and work in the factory with all my friends. I wanted to do something important and be rich by the time I was 21."
 – *Greg Dulli* of **The Afghan Whigs** (1996)

"It's a big mistake to lose your identity just to aspire to something you're never going to get."
 – *Paul Weller,* ex-**The Jam** (1995)

"I'm driven, I am. I'm driven, for some reason. But I don't know where I'm going."
 – *Courtney Love* of **Hole** (1992)

"There is nothing at all the matter with some journalists that a quick slap in the face couldn't sort out."
   – *Elvis Costello* (1995)

"We got slagged in the British press. They said, 'Buffalo Tom like short words that rhyme.'"
   –*Tom Maginnis* of **Buffalo Tom** (1994)

"I was born cool and no yard-dog journalist can tell me otherwise."
   – *Ian McCulloch* of **Echo & the Bunnymen** (circa 1984)

"People said, 'Here's this white guy plagiarizing black music. But I'm not like those people who build their songs around samples. We're writing songs ourselves and playing around them. To me, it's like saying if we brought in a string quartet, we'd be plagiarizing Bach."
   – *Jason Kay* of **Jamiroquai** (1997)

"Rage Against The Machine wasn't supposed to happen, but it did. It happened in the face of critics who had pretty much abandoned the possibility of music to effect change. I think we proved they were wrong."
   – *Zack De La Rocha*, ex-**Rage Against The Machine** (1999)

"There is so much Hatorade being drunk out there. Every magazine, paper, band, etc. is on a Limp hating rampage."
   – *Fred Durst* of **Limp Bizkit** (2001)

"They say I should be doing Shakespeare instead of all this pop-music crap."
   – *Tom Waits* (2000)

"American rock critics and musicians think that once you've thrown a TV through a hotel-room window, that's you for life and you don't actually have a home to go to – you just grow a long beard like ZZ Top and live in a fucking Greyhound bus or something."
   – *Pete Townshend* (2000)

The White Stripes

"I think it's a good, humbling experience to scrub behind your own toilet."
   – *Natalie Merchant* (1995)

"You can't answer back when someone's calling you a wanker. What do you say? 'I'm not a wanker, I'm alright!'"
   – *Bernard Butler* of **New Order** (1998)

"Our generation likes our pain, and if you dare fucking take it away from us, we're going to kill you. We like our pain and we're selling it."
   – *Tori Amos* (1994)

"Truth — it's quite a mystery, isn't it? Everywhere in my life, people find it hard to be truthful. It's a problem. The truth always serves you best, but people seem to have very different ideas about what the truth is."
   – *Joshua Todd* of **Buckcherry** (2001)

"You can only tell the same joke so many times before people get bored, and you can only tell people to fuck off so many times before they get fed up and stop coming back."
   – *Jay Bentley* of **Bad Religion** (2000)

"People need a vent for their feelings. Slam dancing is like a tribal ritual. It's intense, cathartic, rejuvenating, mystical."
   – *Brett Gurewitz,* owner of Epitaph Records (2001)

"There's not enough female voices in popular culture. It's a fucking crime."
   – *Liz Phair* (1997)

"There's no point in being subversive in rock anymore, there's no way you can be – unless you ram a stick of dynamite up your ass."
   – *Kurt Cobain* of **Nirvana** (1992)

"I'd certainly not like to be like a Nick Drake, being dead and not knowing that I was being appreciated on earth! There's a lot of bullshit myths and romance that go around people like Nick Drake. Part of the reason why he was so upset and depressed was that no one was getting his music at the time. It's great that the good stuff wins out, but you'd much prefer if the good out-ed while you alive."
   — *Jimi Goodwin* of the **Doves** (2000)

"I think anger is a really beautiful thing when it's put to work."
   — *Ian MacKaye* of **Fugazi** (1998)

"Without freedom of expression, good taste means nothing."
   — *Neil Young* (circa 1994)

"It'd be stupid for me to sit here and say that there aren't kids who took up to me, but my responsibility is not to them. I'm not a baby sitter."
   — *Eminem* (2000)

"I could never understand this thing about role models, whether you're talking about a basketball player or a politician or rock star. Why should you pattern your life after what they do or say? You don't know them. The way they live their lives may have nothing to do with what you admire in their professional life."
   — *Lars Ulrich* of **Metallica** (1996)

"If anybody has a father at home who beats your fuckin' mother, you need to go home and stomp that motherfucker into the ground."
   — *Coby Dick* of **Papa Roach** (2000)

"I had an unbelievably happy childhood."
— *Michael Stipe* of **R.E.M.** (1992)

"My earliest memory is pretending to be dead. My mum used to step over me while I was laying on the kitchen floor."
— *Siouxsie Sioux* of **Siouxsie and The Banshees** (1993)

"I spent my whole growing up looking at the ground. I'm serious. I would look down all the time, and it's taken me up until the last couple of years to even be able to look at people."
— *Lou Barlow* of **Sebadoh** (1994)

"I was kicked out of Brownies for guarding the door while two of the cool girls raided the cookie jar and took all the money. I was too afraid to tell my parents, so I would wear my Brownie uniform on the days I was supposed to go, and walk around after school for about an hour."
— *Tanya Donnelly* of **Belly** (1995)

"I used to always play on the piano and pretend I was making the musical score for a monster movie. I could make the piano play itself by jamming on the pedals!"
— *Daniel Johnston* (1999)

"I didn't really have much of a great time in grade school, so I like writing about that. I write about it a lot — actually having friends in grade school and having a girlfriend or something back then when you really wanted it. Kids are so cruel sometimes. It's nice to fantasize that they're not."
— *Jack White* of **The White Stripes** (2001)

"I've got this picture of myself climbing on the fence at PS41. I'm wearing green corduroys, a burgundy T-shirt, a green winter knit cap and I've got Puma Clyde's on. I'm that same kind of kid I was back then, I'm happy. I don't need to change that."
— *Adam Horovitz* of **Beastie Boys** (1998)

"As a kid, I was either completely introverted and scared to death of people, or I was pulling my pants down and screaming at the top of my lungs."
  – *Flea* of **The Red Hot Chili Peppers** (1995)

"When I was 12, I decided to become a musician. Physical Graffiti was the first album I ever owned. My stepfather bought that for me."
  – *Jeff Buckley* (1994)

"I was an altar boy for four years. I was never molested, though."
  – *Greg Dulli* of **The Afghan Whigs** (1996)

"I've learned that no matter how fucked up I might feel my life was growing up, my parents did the absolute best that they knew how."
  – *Aaron Lewis* of **Staind** (2001)

"From a very early age, I was in tune with pop radio, and most of this was done driving. We had an old '67 or '65 Buick Le Sabre, and whenever we would drive around, I would actually stick my head right against the speakers in the back and sing along to the music.
  – *Greg Graffin* of **Bad Religion** (1994)

"The first music I literally grew up listening to as a baby was Rodgers and Hart and Cole Porter. Theirs would have been the first songs that I could name. Obviously I didn't know who had written them at the age of two but my mother says that where kids normally liked nursery rhymes, I liked "I've Got You Under My Skin." The fact that my dad was a musician and my mum sold music meant that it was all around and I was immersed in it from an early age."
  – *Elvis Costello* (1994)

"I grew up in a very poor, violent neighborhood about twenty minutes north of Boston. My mom raised me and my sister single-handedly. We had it rough. We were poor. We lived in a three-tenement home with my relatives upstairs. The streets were always filled with sirens and

gunshots and car chases, fights and drugs. I wouldn't change it for the world, but it was a violent, rough upbringing. It was survival."
   – Sully Erna of **Godsmack** (2000)

"When I moved to California as a kid, I had to consciously remember not to say 'y'all.' Basically, having to do that pissed me off a little bit; I always identified with the South in a certain way."
   – David Lowery of **Cracker** (1996)

"I wasn't allowed to listen to the radio. But I made sure I won one in a contest at school. I kept it hidden. The things I went through in childhood definitely had an effect on where I am now."
   – Axl Rose of **Guns N' Roses** (1992)

"Being a kid is so miserable. I think my mind has blanked a lot of it out."
   – Art Alexakis of **Everclear** (2001)

"I grew up as a rebellious kid who was always locked up in his room. When I got out, I wasn't bad – I just didn't know what was right or wrong."
   – Fred Durst of **Limp Bizkit** (1999)

Marilyn Manson   Photo by Rahav Segev/Photopass.com

"I'm amazed to see how backward humans have gone on the evolutionary chart."
   — *Marilyn Manson* (2000)

"All I really care about are the real, deep problems people have. That's the root of entertainment. I don't want to talk to someone about how their plane flight was; I wanna talk to people about the shit that's hurting them deeply."
   — *Ian Sefchick* of **Creeper Lagoon** (2001)

"I get the impression that people from rural areas are idiots."
   — *Chuck Cleaver* of **The Ass Ponys** (2001)

"People are always looking to a pill to solve their problems. It's like, you can't sleep, take a pill. You can't get a boner, take a pill. You can't eat, take a pill. You're feeling depressed, take a pill. It's not even about resolving your problems anymore, it's all about the easy way out."
   — *Matt Embree* of **Rx Bandits** (2001)

"I don't think that people today are any different than they were 1000 years ago. You're hungry, you're tired, you want to fuck. Anything that stops you from getting one of those three things, you get angry or you may betray someone to get it."
   — *Greg Dulli* of **The Afghan Whigs** (1996)

"People are so detached. People are glued to their computers and their 150 channels of cable. And everything is shoved right down your fucking throat. People have lost their minds."
   — *Martyn Leaper* of **The Minders** (2001)

"I much prefer cynics, abusive people. They're funnier, more truthful. Nice guys grow on trees."
   —*J Mascis* of **Dinosaur Jr.** (1993)

"There are certain people out there, you're never going to please 'em, so you might as well piss 'em off."
   — *Peter Holmstrom* of **The Dandy Warhols** (2000)

Eddie Vedder of **Pearl Jam**   Photo by Rahav Segev/Photopass.com

"Sometimes I get a little sad because I look out into that audience and I know it's not going to be there for very long, that the moment is going to be gone."
— *Billy Corgan* of **Smashing Pumpkins** (1996)

"Maybe I wasn't ready for attention to be placed on me, you know? I never knew that someone could put you on the cover of a magazine without asking you, that they could sell magazines and make money and you didn't have a copyright on your face or something."
— *Eddie Vedder* of **Pearl Jam** (2001)

"It was weird watching Appetite For Destruction go up the charts. At first we couldn't believe we even made the Top 100."
— *Slash* of **Guns N' Roses** (1989)

"Fame, on its best day, is kind of like a friendly wave from the stranger by the side of the road. And when it's not so good, it's like a long walk home, all alone, with nobody in when you get there."
— *Bruce Springsteen* (circa 1985)

"When you can spell subpoena without thinking about it, that's when you know you've made it."
— *David Lee Roth* (1997)

"The thing we never wanted as a band was for our personalities, our celebrity as people, to eclipse the music. But that's happened to a degree, especially for me."
— *Michael Stipe* of **R.E.M.** (1995)

"I'd love for my music to be renowned, but I don't have to go with it…I've come too far to be playing for people who don't care."
— *Paul Westerberg,* ex-**The Replacements** (1996)

"I don't want to be recognized, I don't want to be hassled. I just want to play guitar in a rock & roll band."
— *Chrissie Hynde* of **The Pretenders** (1995)

"What is an autograph, anyway? I'm just scribbling something on a piece of paper."
   —*Tommy Stinson* of **The Replacements** (1991)

"I think entertainers have gotten far too much light shone on them in America. They've got far too much of the center stage and are indulged beyond belief, whether they're into excess or ascetics or ending wars or whatever. They're taken so seriously it's ridiculous.
   — *Peter Garrett* of **Midnight Oil** (1993)

"I get really scared when people call me a rock star. I just wanted people to like our music."
   — *Chad Taylor* of **Live** (1994)

"All the shit that's happened is totally insane, because if you ask anybody that knows me, they'd tell you I've had the worst fucking luck. This is all an avalanche of confetti and balloons and kazoos. Before, the party was just an empty room with a bare light bulb on the ceiling. It was pretty bleak."
   — *Beck* (1994)

"I'm famous now because of unhappiness. Your misery is everyone else's entertainment."
   — *Adam Duritz* of **Counting Crows** (1994)

"I think when you become successful it's very easy to step over and become product, and that has never happened and will never happen to me."
   — *Morrissey* (circa 1994)

"Before I was living in a Salvation Army shelter, and now we're having dinner with Madonna. It's completely crazy."
   — *Tim Armstrong* of **Rancid** (1995)

"I can't imagine how people who have a big, giant level of success deal with it because it's already driving me crazy at a real moderate level."
   — *Matthew Sweet* (1995)

"It's kind of hip to complain about success."
  – *Scott Weiland* of **Stone Temple Pilots** (1993)

"When you become a star, you see sides of humanity most people never see. And it can make you feel lonely."
  – *Chris Cornell* of **Soundgarden** (1999)

"Someone said to me before a show the other day, 'Fifteen thousand people at this arena-this is everything you ever dreamed of.' I turned to him and said, 'Correction. It's everything I never dreamed of.'"
  – *Mike Dirnt* of **Green Day** (1995)

"It's surreal. Like I'm gonna wake up and it's gonna be the longest dream I've ever had."
  – *Chester Bennington* of **Linkin Park** (2001)

"There's aspects of [fame] that there's no way you could be ready for. There's no way that you could be ready for being in a grocery store at 10 in the morning and having a bunch of people run up to you and ask you for your autograph."
  – *Jeff Ament* of **Pearl Jam** (1998)

"It blows my mind that we might be the biggest white band ever to come out of Minneapolis. I don't think I'll ever have a good grip on that."
  – *Dave Pirner* of **Soul Asylum** (1995)

"Famous? I was always famous. I was famous in my school; I was famous in my town. What is famous? It's all relative you know?
  – *Sting* (1991)

"When you're humble enough to realize that you are no better than any person, and that your elevated place in the world is due to luck, timing and a record company that profits tenfold compared to what you earn, you feel guilty."
  – *Stephen Malkmus* of **Pavement** (1994)

"We've gotten the same line of questioning for years: "What will you do if you get famous?" And we keep saying it ain't gonna happen."
    – *Steve Turner* of **Mudhoney** (1995)

"I didn't know how to deal with success. If there was a Rock Star 101 course, I would have liked to take it. It might have helped me."
    – *Kurt Cobain* of **Nirvana** (1993)

"The more successful you get, the more opinions you seem to have and the more opinions people have about you. People come up to you in the street saying, 'I really hate that song.' Friends suddenly have ideas for your videos. Distant relatives start getting very interested in you."
    – *Justine Frischmann* of **Elastica** (1995)

"We've got to always remember why the fuck we're here, which is to make music, not to build statues of ourselves, not to start thinking our shit doesn't stink, not to lose ourselves so that it's only vanity that gets our knob moving."
    – *Mike Bordin* of **Faith No More** (1995)

"If we had sold as many records as Pearl Jam or someone years ago, I would have overdosed on something. I would have been a rock casualty for sure."
    – *Al Jourgensen* of **Ministry** (1999)

"I can see why people can't handle fame. You have to be tough as nails. Everybody gets everything wrong about you. I mean, working hard is definitely a relief after years of not working, but I'm burned now. I'm quite edgy. I'm not sure what the future holds. It's all a bit overwhelming and I just need to chill out at home. I wasn't born yesterday, but I didn't realize how cutthroat it was."
    – *Gavin Rossdale* of **Bush** (1996)

"It's a lot better than being thought of as 'Johnny from A Flock of Seagulls."
    – *Johnny Marr,* ex-**The Smiths** (1999)

"Anybody who tells you that, 'Oh, yeah, we only like to play in clubs –
we like this intimate atmosphere' has not played in front of 10,000
people who just totally dig your shit. That's such a rush man. That's a
blast."
     – *David Lowery* of **Cracker** (1996)

"You're catapulted into this position where your ego is blown up to
the size of a major planet. And you begin to believe that you can do
anything. And that might not be a bad thing ultimately, except the poor
public has to suffer through a lot of it."
     – *Michael Stipe* of **R.E.M.** (1992)

"I started getting dressed for gigs, just the whole 'Rambo' thing of
getting prepared and not caring about people who aren't into it. I was
bored of not enjoying it. Now I love it."
     – *Chris Martin* of **Coldplay** (2001)

"I want to feel our success because it's gonna go away. It's not as real
as I thought it was gonna be. Like someone will come up to me and
scream, 'I love you! You're my favorite band in the world! I've been
listening to you for a month!'
     – *Gwen Stefani* of **No Doubt** (1996)

"I don't necessarily know if we want to be rock stars. Over time you
see the faces of all these people transform, and they become all worn
and torn. They go around killing themselves or freebasing until they
end up looking like Mick Jagger. I'm not sure that's the life for me."
     – *Royston Langdon* of **Spacehog** (1995)

"When I was growing up, the punk rock bands I was always attracted
to were very anti-rock star. This was when it was very uncool to live a
decadent lifestyle. So it makes me want to get defensive because now
I've got the big house, and I have a beautiful 22-year-old wife. And I
think, 'Am I one of those stupid rock stars?'"
     – *Art Alexakis* of **Everclear** (2001)

Rivers Cuomo of **Weezer**   Photo by Rahav Segev/Photopass.com

"Once you're selling, like, nine million albums, you're attracting people who aren't really your fans. You start getting the psychos, the people who sit at home and the radio talks to them."
  – *Peter Buck* of **R.E.M.** (1992)

"I'm generally so understood by our fans that it really doesn't particularly bother me that I'm not critically acclaimed."
  – *Martin Gore* of **Depeche Mode** (2001)

"The fans got to be really bad there for a while. Kids would throw beer bottles at us, thinking it was fun to do, and everyone was laughing and stuff. Meantime, we would be looking to smash the guy's teeth in. Paul [Westerberg] used to jump into the crowd and try to pound the guy."
  – *Tommy Stinson*, ex-**The Replacements** (1992)

"You can never tell if your fans will like an album or if they won't and I'm not gonna sit and try to market myself to anybody."
  – *Billie Joe Armstrong* of **Green Day** (2001)

"There's a part of me that's still a fifteen-year old music fan. My fans are wounded nerds everywhere."
  – *Tanya Donnelly* of **Belly** (1995)

"We see these frat guys coming to our shows and I keep thinking, 'These are the guys that I used to be afraid of. These are the guys who used to head butt me for no reason.' Now they're in the front row. We call it the idiot factor."
  – *Bill Janovitz* of **Buffalo Tom** (1994)

"I once admitted on TV that the strangest summer job I ever had was as a scuba diver, who sexed lobsters for a study. Since then the fans picked it up, and began throwing lobsters. Luckily I've never been hit with a live one."
  – *Stephan Jenkins* of **Third Eye Blind** (1999)

"It's really hard for me to talk to fans now. It feels like they're teetering on every word I say."
— *Aaron Lewis* of **Staind** (2001)

"We get a lot of freaks. Ween is like a freak factory."
— *Mickey Melchiondo* of **Ween** (2000)

"This group appeals to people who are isolated in some way. Geographically or socially or sexually or fashion-wise."
— *Mat Osman* of **Suede** (1994)

"I think there are some fans who care about the music, and others who care about the politics of music. We didn't intend to start a scene at all. We're just doing what we do."
— *Rivers Cuomo* of **Weezer** (2001)

"I like those people who come to see me now. They're not aware of my early days, but I'm glad of that. It lifts that burden of responsibility, of having to play everything exactly like it was on some certain record. I can't do that. Which way the wind is blowing, they're going to come out different every time."
— *Bob Dylan* (1998)

"The monster girls, they followed us everywhere! The were really bad, with beards and warts and everything."
— *Dee Dee Ramone* (2001)

"Some of my fans are quite mad. And some of them are quite frightening."
— *Morrissey* (1997)

"The first punk rock show I ever wanted to go to was the Dead Kennedy's, and I had just gotten my driver's license the day before. I wanted to drive there really bad but my parents said, 'No. You can't take the car. It's in a bad area and it's too late.' I really wanted to go and I threw a temper tantrum. I got so angry that they wouldn't even let me go with anyone else 'cause I was acting like such a brat."
  – Steven Malkmus of **Pavement** (1999)

"The first concert I went to was Derek and The Dominos… when I was fifteen or sixteen. Clapton played "Bell Bottom Blues" and he pointed at me! He kinda did a thumbs-up and pointed. Might have been to somebody else, but of course I thought it was me."
  – Eddie Van Halen (1998)

"The first concert I went to without my mom was Tears For Fears. I was probably 13. All I remember was that I smoked a whole pack of cigarettes and promptly threw up everywhere."
  – Dido (2001)

"When I was about 14, I saw the Clash. I was pushed up close, and people were stage-diving, and there was this sort of glorious, happy, violent chaos at work. It was like an indoctrination to the pain of the pit. I guess I was a little bit afraid, but I was also like, 'Well, actually, bring it; I like my bruises.' It was a sweet kind of pain."
  – Stephan Jenkins of **Third Eye Blind** (2001)

"My sister took me to see Bon Jovi and Skid Row when I was about 13. We sat way up high, and there were people throwing up next to me. I drank my first half a beer and got sick the next day."
  – Brandon Boyd of **Incubus** (2001)

"My first concert was ZZ Top in a big, muddy field in Austin, Texas. I got drunk on Boone's Farm apple wine and threw up most of the time."
  – Kathy Valentine of **The Go-Go's** (2001)

Dave Grohl of **The Foo Fighters**   Photo by Rahav Segev/Photopass.com

"Grunge is a good two parts punk, one part metal. Maybe one part punk, one part metal, and the last part divided between psychedelic and retarded."
 – *Kim Thayill* of **Soundgarden** (1996)

"No one seemed to realize that listening to both the Stooges and Aerosmith was uncool. So everyone did and, without notice, a 'new' sound began to evolve. Fueled equally by the irreverent snottiness of the punk camp and the gloss of the more mainstream hard rock heroes, a new music was being born and it was distinctly Seattle."
 – *Daniel House,* owner of C/Z Records (1994)

"Seattle to me was just some rainy city in the Northwest where The Posies and The Young Fresh Fellows came from."
 – *Paul Westerberg,* ex-**The Replacements** (1993)

"I think lumping it all together as grunge is really bogus."
 – *Steve Turner* of **Mudhoney** (1994)

"The first thing I remember of Pearl Jam was hearing 'Alive' on the radio while I was living in Seattle. I pictured Mountain or some serious '70s throwback The music just seemed like classic rock to me, so I pictured the singer being some husky, fuckin' bearded, leather-jacketed Tad type. Big and fat and tortured and scary."
 – *Dave Grohl* of **The Foo Fighters** (2001)

"Seattle bands are basically trying to update the hair-wagging, shit music that I hated in the seventies that made me want to be in a fucking punk rock band."
 – *Steve Albini* of **Shellac** (1993)

"Grunge. Its pretty silly."
 – *Dan Murphy* of **Soul Asylum** (1993)

"It's hard not to be bitter about the success of the Seattle scene. I lost good friends in the process."
 – *Chris Cornell* of **Soundgarden** (1996)

"Grunge is as potent a term as new wave. You can't get out of it. It's going to be passé. You have to take a chance and hope that either a totally different audience accepts you or the same audience grows with you."
  – *Kurt Cobain* of **Nirvana** (1993)

"When I saw Nirvana smashing their guitars and drum kit, I just felt vindicated."
  – *Noodles* of **The Offspring** (2000)

"Everybody kept calling [Kurt] the voice of a generation, but really, I could never figure out what his songs were about."
  – *Dexter Holland* of **The Offspring** (1995)

"We did this show with Nirvana at the Warfield in San Francisco. They plugged in and from the first chord, Kurt flew into the audience. He was surfing the crowd while playing the song. The crowd threw him back onto the stage, and he hit the first line of the vocal. I was like, 'Fuck it, there is no way we can beat that.'"
  – *Thurston Moore* of **Sonic Youth** (1994)

"Nirvana slayed the hair bands. They shot the top off the poodles. All of a sudden, all those bands like Poison, Bon Jovi and Warrant became like Rommel in the desert: overextended, bloated, no more Vaseline. And now they're just rusty tanks in the desert with no gas. Nirvana is going to be remembered for changing the face of rock."
  – *Henry Rollins* (1994)

"Mythologizing Kurt is something he would abhor."
  – *Michael Stipe* of **R.E.M**. (1994)

"Rock has always been the devil's music."
  – *David Bowie* (circa 1988)

"First of all, we want to thank Satan…"
  – *Anthony Kiedis* of **The Red Hot Chili Peppers** (1992),
  upon receiving an MTV Award

"My mom used to tell me when I was a kid, 'If you curse at nighttime,
the devil's going to come to you when you're sleeping.' I used to get
excited because I really wanted it to happen…I wanted it. I wanted it
more than anything."
  – *Marilyn Manson* (1998)

"Beliefs are dangerous. Beliefs allow the mind to stop functioning. A
non-functioning mind is clinically dead. Believe in nothing."
  – *Maynard James Keenan* of **Tool** (circa 1996)

"I am an atheist. In fact, I like wearing my hair in horns, because I love
the idea that some Christian girl might start to think that her favorite
band is, like, satanic or something."
  – *Adrian Young* of **No Doubt** (1996)

"I don't want to deny beliefs or make people turn away from religion,
but I think everybody should have the right to take a look and form
their own opinion, without being forced to believe something."
  – *Scott Stapp* of **Creed** (1999)

"If your work is any more than one dimension, you believe in fairies…
alternate realities make you a good writer."
  – *Tori Amos* (1996)

"Jesus Christ has been followed and preached about for 2,000 years.
And people seriously think that this little group making a fairly
obscure little record called 'Jesus Sucks' is going to do anybody any
harm whatsoever?"
  – *Jim Reid* of **The Jesus And Mary Chain** (1985)

"I have found by going through other religions that this religion of Judaism happens to be the most intelligent. And when you get through the intelligence, you are on your way up the ladder. Because they don't just take care of this world, and they're not talking about the next, either. They're talking about simultaneously being in this world and the other world. We can do that. Heaven on earth."
  — *Perry Farrell* of **Jane's Addiction** (1998)

"I really disagree with a lot of things that the church does — the Christian church. Just religion in general, I see a lot of things that seem off. To me, God is all about love and mercy and compassion, and I don't see a lot of that today."
  — *Jason Wade* of **Lifehouse** (2001)

"I guess everyone looks for something to pray to when you're feeling grateful for your life or feeling down or whatever it is. I'm not really sure what it is that's out there taking care of us, but I have to believe there's some kind of higher power."
  — *Sully Erna* of **Godsmack** (2000)

"I like a spirituality with a God that knows how to take his girl to the dance club, dance all night, have a little drink, kiss the kid when they come back in and go to sleep. God doesn't need a chauffer."
  — *Jeff Buckley* (1994)

"Religion is a corrupt business. Spirituality is something else. Religion is like Coca-Cola, Pepsi Cola, wine. That's not going to help in the desert. Religion is a corrupt institution and we don't trust those."
  — *Carlos Santana* (2000)

"If he'd have known about the way they burnt witches and that, Jesus would have been mad. But if Jesus had seen U2 he would have been very mad indeed. Jesus would throw bottles at U2."
  — *Mark E. Smith* of **The Fall** (1993)

"Think of what you could do with all the money they spend trying to fight drugs. Legalize them. Take the profit and the glamour out of them."
  – *Lou Reed* (1989)

"I loved the whole ritual – tying off, preparing the needle. I'd get off on that. Drugs were what I was good at."
  – *Art Alexakis* of **Everclear** (1996)

"Mushrooms make me too fucking giggly. I just laugh at everything. I don't like to laugh too much."
  – *Eminem* (2000)

"I used to sit up and freebase for five, six days in a row with no sleep. My hair would be all stuck together like somebody had jacked off in it."
  – *Dave Mustaine* of **Megadeth** (1998)

"My first drug experience was sniffing glue. We tried it, and moved on to Carbona. That's why we wrote songs about it. It was a good high, but it gave you a bad high. I guess it destroys your brain cells."
  – *Johnny Ramone* (2001)

"I think drinking and doing drugs are very important."
  – *Mike Dirnt* of **Green Day** (1995)

"I don't want beer. I want heroin. If I was going to drink, it would be whisky and whisky only, and I would drink it until I vomited."
  – *Kelley Deal* of **The Breeders** (1996)

"The whole point about drugs is to wake up and tell the story to your brothers. Nature put 'em here and, as many claim, God is in control of nature. If he wants them here, who am I to argue."
  – *Perry Farrell* of **Jane's Addiction** (1991)

"I'll never stop smoking pot. I'm a drug addict and always fucking will be. I like my pot."
  – *Shaun Ryder* of **The Happy Mondays** (1991)

"We don't do nearly as many drugs as most people think."
  – *Wayne Coyne* of **The Flaming Lips** (1999)

"I haven't actually been full-on drunk since I was a teenager, so it might be better if you asked about drugs. I wouldn't recommend taking LSD as a cure for insomnia or a migraine."
  – *Sam Coomes* of **Quasi** (1999)

"I love getting stoned, it's the best thing in the fucking world."
  – *Thom E. Yorke* of **Radiohead** (1995)

"We're going to carry on drinking our Cold Medinas, taking drugs, and falling on our faces. If people in Britain don't like it, they know what they can do."
  – *Adam Yauch* of **Beastie Boys** (1987)

"When I found drugs, I thought I'd found the greatest thing. All you do is snort this shit up your nose or stick this needle in your arm, and you're a fucking genius."
  – *Flea* of **The Red Hot Chili Peppers** (1995)

"My dad caught me trippin' acid when I was 14 or something. He put me in my room and gave me this book. I opened it and the first thing it said was, 'The nature of the universe is that it wants to do exactly what you want it to do.' And now I play in a rock and roll band and drink with a big heart."
  – *Ian Sefchick* of **Creeper Lagoon** (2001)

"I think that decriminalization of marijuana is crucial. There are a lot of people smoking it over here and I think it's hypocritical, the way all the lawmakers are swilling back gin and port or whiskey and scrutinizing someone who just wants to smoke a spliff. Governments don't

understand that the people who are smoking it are really keeping it together. You know, paying taxes, holding down jobs, raising kids. They think that anyone who's smoking it must be lying in an alleyway in their underwear covered in open sores."
— *Joe Strummer* (2001)

"I did take heroin when I was pregnant, in the very beginning of my pregnancy, otherwise I could have sued the hell out of Vanity Fair."
— *Courtney Love* of **Hole** (1995)

"I heard that your brain stops growing when you start doing drugs. Let's see, I guess that makes me 19."
— *Steven Tyler* of **Aerosmith** (1979)

"I've never had problems with drugs, I've had problems with the Police."
— *Mick Jagger* of **The Rolling Stones** (1999)

"Glue wasn't exactly the Cadillac of drugs. It wasn't so much a drug as it was a substitute for drugs."
— *Dee Dee Ramone* (2001)

"I totally believe that music gets you into a drug lifestyle, because that's exactly what happened with me. I was always wondering, 'Why does everybody sing about getting high?' Then you get high, and you're like, 'Whoa, that's why.'"
— *Lou Barlow* of **Sebadoh** (1996)

"I don't always want to be known as Mike Ness, the recovering dope fiend who got in a lot of trouble."
— *Mike Ness* of **Social Distortion** (1991)

Beastie Boys

Photo by Dominic Episcopo

"Some people in England thought — and still think — that I'm a pile of shit."
    — *Damon Gough* a.k.a. **Badly Drawn Boy** (2000)

"I don't have to be pretentious or fake to impress anyone around me because they all know exactly what I am. A big fake cunt."
    — *John Lydon* of **Public Image Ltd.** (1998)

"You'd have to be a total idiot to say 'I'm the slacker generation guy.' I'd be laughed out of the room in an instant."
    — *Beck* (1994)

"Everyone goes on about the idea of the sensitive artist, but for me that's all bollocks. I can't stand the idea of being a sad, lonely bedside poet. I'd much rather be perceived as loud and arrogant."
    — *Damon Albarn* of **Blur** (1997)

"People have this obsession: They want you to be like you were in 1969. They want you to, because otherwise their youth goes with you, you know?"
    — *Mick Jagger* of **The Rolling Stones** (1987)

"A lot of people think I'm clinically mad."
    — *Morrissey* (1986)

"Everyone's like, 'you're running naked 'cause you think you're so...' and I'm like, 'no man, this is function.' What am I supposed to do? Come out in leather pants and a stylish shirt and a braided beard? I'm not the dude in whatever band. I'm working up here."
    — *Henry Rollins* (2000)

"There have been things we've put out there where we've been joking about something, and ultimately it's been something that ended up being a negative statement, and unfortunately probably had negative ramifications. But we become more aware of ourselves and of our actions. You've got to evolve, I guess."
    — *Mike D* of **Beastie Boys** (2000)

"The very first time I called myself Alice Cooper, with the make-up smeared everywhere, I was wearing a pink clown outfit with furry afro hair. I must've looked like the scariest thing on two legs."
— *Alice Cooper* (1999)

"A lot of people think we're a bunch of bitches. We can handle people yelling gross things at us, or coming and rubbing our backs, but we're not that tough. We do party, though, and we do break laws."
— *Donna R.* of **The Donnas** (2001)

"People have me all wrong. I used to have a good idea of who I was. I was very lonely – profoundly lonely and frustrated. Now it's like I'm not lonely and I'm not particularly frustrated."
— *Lou Barlow* of **Sebadoh** (1996)

"I like to hear crazy rumors. Didn't I die in a car accident? My mom called me about that one – she was really concerned. And then there was the time I raped someone. My mom also called me about that: 'I'm so disappointed in you!' But she doesn't call me about them anymore. I banned her from the internet."
— *Rivers Cuomo* of **Weezer** (2000)

"I think people are always going to think the worst of me. They're ready and willing to cast me into these dark holes, to say that I'm this physically and mentally unstable character. So I have to be careful not to present them with such an easy target."
— *PJ Harvey* (1997)

"I think the biggest misconception about me is that I'm a moron, a drunk who can't put my trousers on."
— *Shane MacGowan*, ex-**Pogues**(1995)

"I don't think there is 'a typical Cure sound.' That would be stereotyping it. Of course, there's always my voice and a heavy bass line, but I can't change my voice and the bass line always seems to be there."
   – *Robert Smith* of **The Cure** (2000)

"I guess it's like folk music, only really loud."
   – *Mark Louris* of **The Jayhawks** describing his band's sound (1995)

"When I was younger I was into punk, and I liked it because it dragged you along with it like a nervous habit. Our music has a little bit of that in it. It creates an atmosphere, and it also has another level of trying to work through all the twangs and pops within it."
   – *Matt Gentling* of **Archers of Loaf** (1998)

"If you play the first Ramones album, one channel is the guitar and one is the bass. You balance it out and it's just such a force. After it was released, all the bands in London started copying the Ramones. They'll deny it, but it's true. I think Johnny Rotten and Sid Vicious told their producers, 'We want our album to sound like the first Ramones album.'"
   – *Marky Ramone* (2001)

"We knew we were rocking but we were afraid maybe there was no more demand for rock. We thought: 'Maybe rock is dead. That's not our fault.' And then Nirvana hit. It turned out everyone wanted to rock. It was such a huge relief."
   – *Nash Kato* of **Urge Overkill** (1993)

"I've never heard Soft Boys' or my influence in anybody. I think probably all it was, was that we were the connection between their generation and the people in the Sixties, because music in the Seventies, on the whole, was in denial or in recovery from what happened in the Sixties. In the Eighties, they were ready for that kind

of thing, and we were revealed to have been the missing link. If you're talking about style – putting it very crudely, we were the link between the Byrds and R.E.M."
  – *Robyn Hitchcock*, ex-**Soft Boys** (2000)

"It's soul music without using Otis Redding's dictionary of soul."
  – *Jason Pierce* of **Spiritualized**, describing his band's sound (1998)

"We don't play party music."
  – *Chris Cornell* of **Soundgarden** (1996)

"There's a real melancholy in [Abba's] songs... all the flourishes, like big double octaves on the piano, we stole them like crazy."
  – Elvis Costello (1991)

"When The Smiths came on "Top Of The Pops" for the first time, that was it for me. From that day on I wanted to be Johnny Marr."
  – Noel Gallagher of **Oasis** (2000)

"You know, Nick Drake was the very best of all."
  – Tom Verlaine of **Television**

"When you think about Led Zeppelin and Bob Marley, they dogged those people, but when you think about them now, they're our heroes."
  – Lenny Kravitz (1993)

"I liked rockabilly and doo-wop. I came to Roy Orbison really early too. And when I tell people I liked watching Ricky Nelson, they say 'what, you liked Ricky Nelson?' And I say, 'well, James Burton's in the back!' You'd always get to hear one of these amazing solos and I'd wonder how the hell he did it? That's one of the reasons I learnt to play guitar – to be able to play like that."
  – Lou Reed (2000)

"I have this huge catalog of melodies in my head, and I've heard it all, the Merseybeat thing, late '60s psychedelic, glam rock, prog rock. I was there for it all. So that's all part of me, Guided by Voices' name refers to all those influences. That's what the 'voices' are."
  – Bob Pollard of **Guided By Voices** (2001)

"I get that tingle when I listen to Joy Division or The Smiths. There was something really weird going on with those bands, they created their own rules and life and aura."
  – Jimi Goodwin of the **Doves** (2000)

"We came from punk and that wasn't very funny. Johnny Rotten was very funny in interviews, but The Clash weren't funny. And the immediate aftermath of punk, Joy Division and that funereal, fuguelike music, that was the music we came out of."
  – *Bono* of **U2** (2000)

"I was never into punk rock. I liked Blondie, but all that other New York stuff, like Talking Heads never rang true for me. I grew up on 70's radio. Cheap Trick were the ultimate band."
  – *Billy Corgan* of **Smashing Pumpkins** (1996)

"When I was a teenager, I loved the Buzzcocks, Generation X, Elvis Costello. If you look at what those artists sold, they weren't selling big in a world full of hack artists that were selling millions and millions of records."
  – *Matthew Sweet* (2001)

"I hear a lot of stories where kids say that one day they heard Kiss and they were dancing in front of a mirror with a broom. That never happened to me. It was classical music that really touched me."
  – *Jon Crosby* of **Vast** (2000)

"I remember the first record that was given to me – my dad gave me the Eagles' The Long Run. I didn't really care for it too much, but it got me going, you know, it started me."
  – *Josh Todd* of **Buckcherry** (2001)

"I started off, like most kids, with my father's record collection. He had a lot of country and western and some other interesting stuff. I first got really into the Beatles, and then I got really, really into punk in like '82. I was into nothing but punk rock until I was about sixteen. I had a fanzine and a little punk label that put out 45s. Later, when Ween had been together for a while, we got really into drugs and my musical tastes changed. I got really into Zeppelin and Hendrix. So I was into punk rock shit, classic rock shit and avant-garde shit, like the Butthole Surfers."
  – *Mickey Melchiondo* of **Ween** (2000)

"I thought metal was stupid Iron Maiden and all that bullshit. I was a Stooges guy, I was a Sabbath guy, and all that high vocal stuff started making me sick. Like, 'What is this, a buncha girls?'"
   – *Dave Wyndorf* or **Monster Magnet** (2001)

"AC/DC's 'Highway To Hell' is the greatest meshing of vocal, guitar and content I've ever heard. That's what I aspire to."
   – *Bonnie Raitt* (2000)

"I've discovered the Beach Boys in just the past year or so, and I have an obsession. I actually just got an import of Smiley Smile and it has Brian Wilson having a breakdown on tape. But it's pretty amazing – here's this musical genius who has no idea what's going on."
   – *Warren Fitzgerald* of **The Vandals** (2000)

"My role models from an early age were people I knew, not people I heard on records – people who weren't driven by record sales or material rewards, they were driven by art itself. I don't know any other way to do it."
   – *Steve Earle* (2000)

"I'm not the greatest songwriter, yet; I daydream thinking about great songwriters. I was brought up with all these different influences – Nina Simone, Nusrat Fateh Ali Kahn, Patti Smith – people who showed me music should be free, should be penetrating, should carry you."
   – *Jeff Buckley* (1994)

"Probably the one person who made me to do this job was Bon Scott from AC/DC. His lyrics were very rebellious. When I listen to that record now, it really reminds me of when I was a kid, standing in my room headbangin' to AC/DC."
   – *Stuart Cable* of **The Stereophonics** (2001)

"We've grown up with Kurt Cobain as well as Rage and Aerosmith, The Pistols and The Stones. We've watched all that, historically, then arrived at our own conclusions."
   – *Keith Nelson* of **Buckcherry** (2001)

"I love old metal, but I also love The Beatles and Radiohead. That synthesis is where it all happens. People hear our records and realize it's not eleven versions of the same song. It' s gonna be diverse, simply because I'll listen to Pantera and then I'll throw on Emmylou Harris."
   – *Carl Bell* of **Fuel** (2000)

"If it wasn't for The Ramones, or Joey in particular, there wouldn't be a Green Day, an Offspring, a Rancid, a Blink 182 – there wouldn't be any punk band, period. There are bands that are influenced by the Ramones that don't even know it yet."
   – *Billie Joe Armstrong* of **Green Day** (2001)

"The Ramones, and specifically Joey, were probably the most significant musical force for people like me, who were disaffected geeks in the early Seventies and didn't have any relationship to disco and overblown rock. Joey was six feet six and skinny, with what my grandfather used to call a subway tan – just super pale – and he was the lead singer. I mean, the lead singer was supposed to be Robert Plant."
   – *Thurston Moore* of **Sonic Youth** (2001)

"I should be sending Pete Townshend cards for Father's Day."
   – *Eddie Vedder* of **Pearl Jam** (1995)

"The Sex Pistols on TV were more violent and crazy than Kiss. It made me want to go into my room and break everything…and then I did."
   – *Jesse Malin* of **D Generation** (1996)

"Iggy Pop was the most hated man in rock & roll. At his early gigs, all the jocks in the audience hated his fucking guts. And I like that, man.
   – *Vinnie Dombrowski* of **Sponge** (1995)

"I grew up listening to a lot of prog rock – most people don't like prog rock at all – but I think there are some good ones. I did listen to a few that now I realize are terrible. The ones that I actually loved I

still like. But say, like, Genesis is pretty slim pickin's as far as the good records go."
   – *Sam Coomes* of **Quasi** (1999)

"There's no denying our metal roots, but we're also into everything from The Beatles to Pink Floyd to Hank Williams. We pop all our ideas in a mixing bowl and see what comes out."
   – *Jerry Cantrell* of **Alice In Chains** (1993)

"Our teachers were Thunders, Chilton, The Faces, The Stones, The Pistols, The Ramones and all the other people who were basically fuck-ups."
   – *Paul Westerberg,* ex-**The Replacements** (1991)

"When they make lists of classic albums, they never mention black music, and they never talk about disco music. I love disco. It and club music were the two most innovative forms of music in the '70s, y'know, it wasn't rock music."
   – *Bobby Gillespie* of **Primal Scream** (1999)

"I remember really being interested in what I was seeing in Creem magazine and buying Fun House by The Stooges. It was so mono-dynamic compared to everything else that was around. I'd play it for friends and they'd take it off and put on Deep Purple's Machine Head."
   – *Thurston Moore* of **Sonic Youth** (circa 1994)

"Great hip-hop is some of the most exciting music you can find. It's certainly more entertaining per pound than alternative rock. The KRS-One/Boogie Down Productions stuff, to me, that's the best shit on the planet."
   – *Page Hamilton* of **Helmet** (1994)

"I've always been a huge Cure fan, especially when Robert Smith was really abstract and cryptic, like in Pornography, where the lyrics were really cryptic, but definitely intense and everybody understood and felt what he was trying to say."
   – *Chino Moreno* of **The Deftones** (2000)

"The first band I ever felt a part of were The Jam. I was a teenager and they were the best group in England. Paul Weller was the coolest pop singer. Totally. The Jam always had a single out every three months, which is what Oasis are trying to emulate."
  – *Noel Gallagher* of **Oasis** (1994)

"I'd listen to Velvet Underground records when I was in high school, and it didn't make me want to go and stick my head under a truck. It made me totally stronger."
  – *Kim Thayil* of **Soundgarden** (1996)

"I've never been a really big rock fan. Motown, anonymous northern soul records, hip-hop, house, that's what moves me."
  – *Mani* of **The Stone Roses** (1994)

"I have two heroes, John Lennon and Stevie Wonder. Asking me where I heard of them first is like asking me where I heard about oxygen. They're just there. As far as my world is concerned they are two of the elements which make up the physical universe."
  – Jake Slichter of **Semisonic** (2001)

"Elton John has got a fucking great voice, and you just can't deny it. He can sing his ass off, and he can play. I love all his shit, man – 'Bennie and the Jets,' 'Daniel,' all his slow shit."
  – *Kid Rock* (2000)

"Kiss had changed my world. It seemed evil and scary – the embodiment of rebelliousness when you're age 12 and starting to get hair on your balls."
  – *Trent Reznor* of **Nine Inch Nails** (1995)

"I thought Johnny Thunders was cool and Keith Richards; that's why I wanted to be a junkie guitar player."
  – *Mike Ness* of Social Distortion (1993)

"You've gotta be true to your roots, only thing is mine are all over the place: The Residents, Rush, Larry Graham, Tony Levin. What frustrates me is the narrow-minded people who only have roots here or there. And how many bands are making shitloads of money by sounding like Alice In Chains, Pearl Jam and Nirvana?"
   – *Les Claypool* of **Primus** (1993)

"I'm the first to admit that we were totally dependent on a particular place and time… for us, seeing Minor Threat at the CBGB hardcore matinee was just as necessary a force in our lives as the Treacherous Three at Club Negril, or the Funky Four + One More at the Rock Lounge."
   – *Mike D.* of **Beastie Boys** (1992)

"I think Camel cigarettes are a big influence on my voice."
   –*Greg Dulli* of **The Afghan Whigs** (1993)

"When The Pixies' *Doolittle* came out, I was working a suit-and-tie job. On my lunch hour I saw the cassette on sale. I threw it in my Walkman, started walking back to work. I got to the corner, called in sick, took a bus all over San Francisco for hours listening to that album over and over. When I got home, I told my wife, 'Look, this is bullshit. I'm starting a band tomorrow.'"
   – *Art Alexakis* of **Everclear** (1996)

"I was really into Iron Maiden. I can remember when I first laid eyes on the great three-story-high Iron Eddie puppet. It was pretty impressive, especially when you're on cheap weed, cheap scotch and No Doz."
   – *Marcus Durant* of **Zen Guerilla** (2001)

"When we took bands like Mudhoney and Nirvana on tour, bands that admitted having been influenced by us, we in turn were being influenced by them. That was why Dirty reached a certain point of being really heavy sounding."
   – *Thurston Moore* of **Sonic Youth** (1995)

"Billy Joel's "Piano Man" was the most influential record of my life."
— *Jim Ward* of **At The Drive In** (2000)

"Hearing The Go-Go's album Beauty and the Beat was a total revelation for me. And then I proceeded to listen to it about 6,000 times, you know, on my headphones, in my bedroom, looking out the window, just fantasizing about being Belinda Carlisle, or Jane Wiedlin. I just loved them."
— *Nina Gordon* of **The Cardigans** (2000)

"The first rock show that kicked my ass was in junior high school, when I saw Kiss play in a theater in Dayton called the Palace. I just couldn't believe it. This is before they had bombs and shit onstage. I think maybe Gene Simmons spit blood, but I thought he cut himself on a whiskey bottle. That kicked my ass and that was the thing that convinced me to get a band."
— *Bob Pollard* of **Guided By Voices** (2001)

"Of course we are big fans of Roxy Music. Inside the first album, Roxy Music, you learn what a really cool '70s rock & roll outfit means. Platform boots, tight jacket. Wahoo!"
— *Jean-Benoit Dunckel* of **Air** (2001)

"The Suicidal Tendencies' debut album, I listened to that for so long when I was young. That song "Institutionalized" is a classic song. I felt like Mike Muir because I had parents telling me I was crazy for what I did."
— *Fred Durst* of **Limp Bizkit** (1999)

"I loved Midwestern 7-Eleven parking lot rock. That's what I was all about as a 13-year old."
— *Tom Morello* of **Rage Against The Machine** (1996)

"I like Fugazi as much as I like AC/DC as much as I like Nick Drake. And I am utterly fascinated by Destiny's Child. No shit."
— *Jim Adkins* of **Jimmy Eat World** (2001)

"If I could see one band that I never got to see, it would be Stiff Little Fingers. They were one of the first punk rock bands I ever heard, and they're partially responsible for me even playing guitar."
   – *Tom DeLonge* of **Blink 182** (2001)

"When I was growing up I thought Kim Deal was the most brilliant woman in rock."
   – *Shirley Manson* of **Garbage** (1996)

Thom Yorke of **Radiohead**   Photo by Rahav Segev/Photopass.com

"Records which inspire people – whether it be to hate the music or love it – are the only kinds of records to make."
   – Rob Dickinson of **The Catherine Wheel** (1993)

"I think OK Computer was a song too long. With our music, forty-five minutes is enough. That's all the human ear can take."
   – Ed O'Brien of **Radiohead** (2001)

"We don't subscribe to traditional definitions of good sound quality."
   *– Calvin Johnso*n of **Beat Happening** (1991)

"When we recorded [Hello Nasty] we always wore the short shorts, the long socks and the shin pads. That way the creative vibe was just so."
   – Mike D. of **Beastie Boys** (2000)

"Those [early songs] were great but it was absolute murder recording them. At one point, during "Dedicated Follower of Fashion," Ray took a whole spool of tape, tipped it on the studio floor and set fire to it.
   – Peter Quaife of **The Kinks** (1998)

"My records are not just cost efficient but time efficient. I'm not part of the Kate Bush/Bryan Ferry school of lingering in the studio. I like to do things in one and a half takes. I think that a song has an essential feel – you either get that or you don't.
   – Robyn Hitchcock (1995)

"The studio is an instrument, manipulate it, don't go in thinking it's got to sound like my band. When I got done with *Pretty Hate Machine*, I realized, 'Holy fuck, how am I going to play this live?'"
   – Trent Reznor of **Nine Inch Nails** (1996)

"I enjoy multi-track recording very much, but I feel like we're just scratching the surface with the live two track. It's not what we can do with it, it's the atmosphere, the feeling. It doesn't matter if we're doing something that sounds really slick, or something that sounds really

raw and punk rock. It's more about the feeling for what it's like to be in the studio, and everyone playing at the same time, just getting rid of the tedium factor for the most part."
    – Frank Black (2001)

"I have a serious political objection to ProTools because it enables someone who can't play in time or sing to sound like fuckin' Queen. I think there's something wrong with that. I think it says a lot about how you look being more important that how you play."
    – John Davis of **Superdrag** (2001)

"I make records unconsciously. I make records because I enjoy the sound of them, because I enjoy the process. It's only when you get to this stage that you have to work out why you do it, how you do it and if there's some sort of meaning behind it. I don't know the answer yet but it's good to talk."
    – Sting (2000)

"The records I make probably won't be listened to in ten years' time. That's all right; I'll just make some more."
    – Fatboy Slim (2000)

"As much as I love making records, I do feel a certain amount of guilt, firstly, being part of a consumer society, and, second, generating all this plastic and bleached paper. I figure if I'm going to make CDs, I might as well try and communicate something that at least I think is important, for, to, people."
    – Moby (2001)

"It's not fucking rocket science."
    – Thom Yorke of **Radiohead** (2001)

"I feel like an asshole throwing a TV through a wall when the money I paid to do that could feed a family for a month. A lot of money can fuck you up bad, man."
     – *Jerry Cantrell* of **Alice In Chains** (1991)

"I don't feel guilty for being rich and famous."
     – *Sting* (1996)

"I've had a grounded life since the Clash. I haven't been lying in the Bahamas."
     – *Joe Strummer* (2001)

"You know, Mozart and Beethoven never got royalty checks."
     – *Joe Walsh* (1997)

"If we make a pisspot full of money, I'm ready to buy a Cadillac and eat caviar."
     – *Dale Crover* of **The Melvins** (1994)

"I want our records to sell a million copies. I want to make as much money as Phil Collins."
     – *William Reid* of **The Jesus and Mary Chain** (1993)

"I've never been a rich guy before. I don't know the rules, so it's been really fun. Making money playing music. It's the best possible thing in the world."
     – *Matt Cameron* of **Pearl Jam** (1998)

"Financially, I want to be big in America, because that means I'll never have to work again. But it's not important to me to be a big star. It's more important to be big in England, because that's where I live, that's where I come from."
     – *Noel Gallager* of **Oasis** (1996)

"I used to work in jobs I hated because I needed the money to buy a guitar. I know what it feels like to have money, to be successful, to be

independent, but I can tell you that money and success never solve your problems."
    – Chris Cornell of **Soundgarden** (1999)

"Money comes in – great! We can let the good times roll, we can have fun with it. But if you start out and get caught up in the idea that these things are going to sustain you in some fashion when you get 20 years down the road, you're gonna be in for a surprise."
    – Bruce Springsteen (1996)

"Once I had all the time in the world and no money. Now I have the money, but no time."
    – John Paul Jones of **Led Zeppelin** (1994)

"I think the amount of money we make shouldn't be any gauge. The main thing I'm concerned with is putting out music that's consistent with what we've done in the past. Doing it our way. That's what it's all about."
    – Greg Graffin of **Bad Religion** (1996)

"Somebody said to me, 'But The Beatles were anti-materialistic.' That's a huge myth. John and I literally used to sit down and say, 'Now, let's write a swimming pool.'"
    – Paul McCartney (1983)

"We've always done it for the money."
    – Mick Jagger of **The Rolling Stones** (1989)

"There's a million screwed up people. You can easily do something really fucked up and sell a million records."
— *Rob Zombie* of **White Zombie** (1995)

"Every rebellion is co-opted and in 50 years is seen as a natural progression from what came before."
— *Stephen Malkmus* of **Pavement** (1994)

"I can't be Bjork, I can't be PJ Harvey, and I can't be Courtney Love. I am who I am. Maybe I limit myself in how comfortable I feel about my body. Maybe I'm just too inhibited. I don't have any tattoos or pierced private parts, but at the same time I've been able to endure over a decade under a great amount of scrutiny."
— *Natalie Merchant*, ex-**10,000 Maniacs** (1995)

"I'm a lot more interested in doing something that can be misinterpreted. Ambiguity has a certain power to involve people."
— *J Robbins* of **Jawbox** (1994)

"I question everything constantly. You have to be able to change all the time, because things change."
— *John Lydon* of **Public Image Ltd.** (1991)

"It's all right letting your self go, as long as you can get your self back."
— *Mick Jagger* of **The Rolling Stones** (1994)

You gotta be really careful what you bite off. Don't bite off more than you can chew. It's a dangerous world."
— *Ozzy Osbourne* (1998)

"I think it's your own choice if you turn from an angry young man to a bitter, old bastard, or if you stay hungry in a good way."
— *Billie Joe Armstrong* of **Green Day** (2000)

"Your shoes have got to match what color guitar you're playing. I had this black guitar and I was going, 'Gem, I can't seem to dress with this guitar."
 – *Noel Gallagher* of **Oasis** (2000)

"Don't ever water your shit down. Do exactly what you do, never compromise, have a fucking good time and look good doing it, man."
 – *Courtney Taylor* of **The Dandy Warhols** (2000)

"Some people are very cerebral and can dream a little. We do manual labor."
 – *Jay Farrar* of **Son Volt** (1995)

"This whole thing about how we've remained successful over a long period of time, the answer's so simple. The songs, if the songs weren't good, we could have the best look, the best attitude, but it would mean nothing."
 – *Robert Smith* of **The Cure** (1996)

"The only credo I have is, 'never give up.' It's when you're at your lowest that you really need some sort of credo, innit? It's really useful in the darkest hour. Besides it's only three words long and you can't fucking forget it."
 – *Joe Strummer* (2001)

"I never swear on my mother's life. I don't think it's a nice thing to do."
 – *Shane MacGowan* (1995), formerly of **The Pogues**

"I had a shrink when I was in the nuthouse, and he gave me one good rule that's stuck with me. He said, 'Before you do anything, ask yourself; am I going to get away with it?"
 – *Iggy Pop*

"I never said I wanted to be around for a long time. I always said I wanted to be here for a good time."
 – *Kid Rock* (1999)

"If I started thinking too much about how influential I've been, then I'd be more of a turd than I already am."
   – *Iggy Pop* (1993)

"Maybe I'm not easy to work with but there has to be somebody who knows the direction. Anarchy in a band just doesn't work."
   – *Robert Smith* of **The Cure** (2000)

"I am a perfectionist. Some even claim that I'm a terror, a dictator and they're right. But I'm also talented and I know when I create something great."
   – *Lou Reed* (1998)

"I can't play long solos anymore without boring myself."
   – *Eric Clapton* (2001)

"I'm not a genius – I've just written songs since I was a kid and I've gotten good at it."
   – *Bob Pollard* of **Guided By Voices** (2001)

"I'm playing the three chords I know, and playing them badly. I'm the type of guy who learned to play guitar from Ramones records, so I learned some really bad habits."
   – *Mark McGrath* of **Sugar Ray** (2001)

"I don't think I have a style. I think a style is the ability to be instantly recognizable and yet have very few variations in what you do. And I don't think I've got a style in that sense because there isn't one thing that I always defer to. There are people with a very definite style and it's like a thread. I think of Van Morrison as someone with a definite style. [John] Lennon was maybe another one but I don't think I'm like that."
   – *Elvis Costello* (2000)

"I don't exist. Tap my head and it sounds like metal. I walk across the sun and I don't cast a shadow."
   – *Brett Anderson* of **Suede** (1994)

"Have you ever read that Little Richard autobiography? He's born again now, but he's absolutely glad and absolutely unrepentant about all the things he's done. Me too."
— *Lloyd Cole* (2000)

"I've been disappointed with some of my work, but I do like an awful lot of it, I'm afraid. My one problem is that I'm not very consistent."
— *David Bowie* (1999)

"If everybody vanishes, if everybody decides tomorrow morning that I'm an impossible ass, then that's fine. You know, if the president of RCA says, 'Fuck Dave Matthews' — great. It would run off my back."
— *Dave Matthews* (2001)

"I'm as stupid as the next person."
— *Van Morrison* (1989)

"I'm obsessed with the thing that makes somebody hurt somebody else. It's something I will never be able to resolve, and it's everywhere."
— *Tanya Donnelly* of **Belly** (1995)

"I'm barely prolific and incredibly lazy."
— *Tom Petty* (circa 1989)

"I've wasted a lot of time looking for that pen I lost. Dollar thirty-nine fucking pisses me off, man; I'll turn over tables looking for that thing. Yeah, I get into stuff. If I get into some writer, I want to read everything, the notes, what he wrote on the back of a napkin. Whatever."
— *Henry Rollins* (2000)

"I'm naïve in a Luke Skywalker way. Not intuitive or smart enough to be a Darth Vader."
— *Ryan Adams* of **Whiskeytown** (2001)

"I'll take advice, I'm a reasonable guy. But if it comes down to what you want and what I want, I'm going to win."
  – *Greg Dulli* of **The Afghan Whigs** (1994)

"I can explore my sick mind, I can explore my love mind, I can explore my dark mind. I have homicidal thoughts and maybe that's one part of the day, and then in another part of the day I just want to be in love. And then I see a porno, and I'm just like, yeah, I just want to get in there and, you know, get physical."
  – *Joshua Todd* of **Buckcherry** (2001)

"Perhaps I'm a bit claustrophobic psychologically. I hate to be trapped. No one's yet come up to me with a limit. They've tried, but I've always been able to duck and weave and I'm still doing that."
  – *Sting* (1993)

"I'm a bit of a pain to work with. I have a particular vision of how it should be, and you have to go along with that."
  – *Mick Jones,* formerly of **The Clash** (1994)

"I still think of myself as an awkward tomboy. It's something I'll never get over, no matter how many magazines I'm in."
  – *Jewel* (1998)

"I'm less and less polite as the years wear on."
  –*Tanya Donnelly* of **Belly** (1995)

"Don't you think it's about time I grew up? I'm 43-years old, man."
  – *Bob Pollard* of **Guided By Voices** (2001)

"When my life gets really fucked up, I get really intense emotional experiences. It's like a manic-depressive elevator with two buttons."
  – *Courtney Taylor* of **The Dandy Warhols** (2000)

"I'm just a very well-paid juvenile delinquent."
  – *Al Jourgensen* of **Ministry** (1999)

"My karma could've been to be born in some poverty-stricken slum somewhere in the world with no chance and instead I'm born with a lot of things in my favor. And still I'm able to screw things up pretty good."
— *Chris Isaak* (1995)

"I'm just a regular guy, you know? There's no leotard and cape under my clothes. I shit, I piss, I drink too much and throw up, just like everybody else."
— *Chester Bennington* of **Linkin Park** (2001)

"I knew that at some point, the true me would come out. I repressed it for quite a long time and that is perhaps why a lot of the anger is more overt. Before, I was nice out of respect or fear or worrying about not getting someone's approval because I objected to something. Now, I can just sort of exorcise my demons."
— *Alanis Morissette* (1995)

"I'm just a regular motherfucker. I'm Marshal Mathers before I'm Slim Shady, before I'm Eminem, before I'm anybody."
— *Eminem* (2000)

"I've got a pretty bad temper sometimes, but who the fuck doesn't? You're getting fucked with, and you do get fucked with everyday – everybody does – at some point you just snap and kill somebody. Ha ha ha. Just kidding."
— *Mark Lanegan* of **Screaming Trees** (1993)

"I do things to amuse myself. Like Madonna, I always need to reinvent myself when I get bored."
— *Scott Weiland* of **Stone Temple Pilots** (1994)

"Perhaps I'm unique because people are so dull. I'm not very good at being dull."
— *Morrissey* (1991)

"I guess I do have a violent side. I hope it's under control these days. But, yeah, I'm an extremist."
    – *Neil Young* (circa 1988)

"I still don't know who the fuck I am. I know what I don't believe in. I know what I've rejected. But I don't know what I do believe in."
    – *Trent Reznor* of **Nine Inch Nails** (1995)

"I am sweet, but fuck with me and I'll wipe the floor with you."
    – *Shirley Manson* of **Garbage**

"I hid behind using the guitar as a machine gun. And it kept me safe. I've never been beaten up, and that's a good thing to say when you're a man. And maybe, as I'm becoming a frail old fellow, it's probably not a very good time to shove it off, and I probably will get beat up next week."
    – *Pete Townshend* (2001)

"I'm very down-to-earth, I have to make sure there's bread and electricity – I'm that kind of practical girl."
    – *Bjork* (1998)

"I'm probably one of the nicest people I've ever met – I'm very smart, very witty. I'm a little cocky, too. No one ever gets a gibe in at me. I'm too fast, too good with my mouth."
    – *Kid Rock* (2000)

"You can't go around taking your dick out. Some people don't like it."
    – *Anthony Kiedis* of **The Red Hot Chili Peppers** (1993)

"For a 6-foot-3 guy with no hair and a whiny voice, I've done alright."
    – *Billy Corgan* of **Smashing Pumpkins** (1999)

"Am I bonkers? No, it's just the rest of the world."
    – *Matt Johnson* of **The The** (1993)

Joe Strummer

Photo by Jason Homa

It used to be that we'd go out for three weeks and come home for three weeks. Now we go out for three weeks and go home for like a week. But even that week helps. You can re-group and get it together to get ready for another one. A lot of bands tour for a few years at a time, but they play for an hour and they don't drink and they don't jump. And they don't rock like we do."
   – *Bob Pollard* of **Guided By Voices** (2001)

"We only tour so that we can shop in different cities. The rest is just an adjunct. And that's no lie."
   – *Lee Ranaldo* of **Sonic Youth** (2000)

"I love being on tour. I totally live to tour and explore the world."
   – *Evan Dando* of **The Lemonheads** (1996)

"Spending so much time on the road, I get to fart all the time. Then when it's, like, Thanksgiving dinner and I'm sitting with my grand-mother, I can't fart for, like, two hours."
   – *Tom DeLonge* of **Blink 182** (2001)

"A lot of rock clubs, which is where I play, are just designed to sell beer and let people urinate."
   – *Frank Black* (2001)

"It's just so fucking boring out there on the road. I just kind of mope around. If I was home, I'd probably be sitting down on the couch with a forty and a Twinkie. Now, it's, like, I get into these hotel rooms, and I gotta call room service to order a forty and a Twinkie."
   – *Uncle Kracker* (2001)

"I wake up early, have a triple latte and head straight to the gym to work out for a few hours. Then it's time for sound check. After that, I go to the gym backstage. I do some cardio, take a couple shots of espresso and I'm good to go."
   – *Boyd Tinsley* of **The Dave Matthews Band** (2001)

"A lot of people don't like the road, but it's as natural to me as breathing. I do it because I'm driven to do it, and I either hate it or love it. I'm mortified to be on the stage, but then again, it's the only place where I'm happy."
  – *Bob Dylan* (1997)

"You tend to wallow when you're on tour because you look out the window and you're missing every day life. It's hard to make anything last out there."
  – *Paul Westerberg,* ex-**The Replacements** (1996)

"I love my job. I love the position I'm in. I love all the benefits that come with it, but I still hate touring."
  – *Michael Stipe* of **R.E.M.** (1994)

"Touring's the greatest job you could have. Not only do you get to wear the same clothes all the time, but you work for just six weeks and then you're off."
  – *Lou Barlow* of **Sebadoh** (1999)

"There isn't a town in the world I haven't run amok in."
  – *Joe Strummer* (1999)

"On our last tour, Donna C. and I were single, so we started a make out contest. I won and the score was five to one. It was cool to pick the cutest guy in the club and just say, 'I'm gonna make out with that one,' and go do it."
  – *Maya Ford* a.k.a. Donna F. of **The Donnas** (2000)

"If you toured with a backpack, a dog, and a Winchester, that would be really fun. But on a bus with nine other men, looking out the window just to notice that you've crossed the border of Idaho and your treat every day is to get off at Junior's Truck Stop and eat something really sugary – then you wouldn't want to do it, no matter how many groupies would suck your dick."
  – *Robert Sledge* of **The Ben Folds Five** (1999)

"I'm very healthy and natural when it comes to sex. Strange locations always turn me on. Aeroplane toilets. I think that would turn anybody on."
    – *Bjork* (1996)

"I'm not homosexual and I'm not heterosexual. I'm... sexual."
    – **Michael Stipe** of **R.E.M.** (1994)

"I think about giving head, though. I don't know why I'm saying this, but I think about that. I'd be good at giving head... I mean no one knows how to jack yourself off better than yourself, you know?"
    – *Trent Reznor* of **Nine Inch Nails** (1995)

"I've never taken advantage of one night stands. It's like treating sex like sneezing. Sex is a fairly disgusting sort of tufted, smelly-area kind of activity, which is too intimate to engage in with strangers."
    – *Thom Yorke* of **Radiohead** (1995)

"I'll tell you what's fun: finding the right stewardess and turning her upside-down in the back of the plane. Ever done it? You come so fast."
    – *Steven Tyler* of **Aerosmith** (1994)

"Music is a lot like sex. If you're having sex with someone who doesn't inspire you, then what are you doing it for?"
    – *Natalie Merchant*, ex-**10,000 Maniacs** (1995)

"You've got to be able to fuck to it – if you can't fuck to it your album sucks."
    –*Tripp Lamkins* of **The Grifters** (1994)

"Even if you have only two seconds, drop everything and give him a blow job. That way, he won't really want sex with anyone else."
    – *Jerry Hall,* ex-wife of *Mick Jagger* (1999)

"We have one roadie who has a panty fetish, and he collects them. He has an anvil case full of them."
    – *Stephan Jenkins* of **Third Eye Blind** (1998)

"I see myself as a bisexual man who's never had a homosexual experience."
  – *Brett Anderson* of **Suede** (1993)

"It was seedy and horrible. We got to it so quickly that I didn't get time to take off my socks, and there's nothing very erotic about getting your virginity taken when you've got your socks on and so has he."
  – *Shirley Manson* of **Garbage** (1996)

"I'm pretty sure that nuns must have sexual feelings and desires, and I reckon that they must find Christ up on that cross incredibly sexy. They must have a lot of masturbatory fantasies about Jesus."
  – *Bobby Gillespie* of **Primal Scream** (2000)

"I had so much sexual guilt in my early twenties that I had 23 bladder infections in one year."
  – *Tori Amos* (1996)

"As far as I'm concerned, the church has no right to open up it's mouth about sex for these reasons: none of them have ever had sex, the second reason is that they do have sex."
  – *Sinead O'Connor* (2000)

"Everybody wants me to carry the gay flag. My sexuality was not a choice, and people have wanted to make an issue of this. I'm not a freak. I'm a human being. I'm a writer. I've never understood the gay lifestyle. It's not part of what makes me a person. If I decide to have sex with a man, I'm not sure that I absolutely have to be a gay role model."
  – *Bob Mould*, of **Sugar**, ex-**Husker Du** (1994)

"Masturbation is a great thing to talk about, I love to bring it up whenever I first meet people."
  – *Mike Patton* of **Faith No More** (1995)

"The other night, this guy gave me head. I'm not gay. I don't think so, anyway. I don't know. I just wanted to see what it felt like. And you know, he stunk. I thought 'it's gonna be good, because he's a guy.' He went at it like he was eating corn on the cob or something."
  – *Perry Farrell* of **Jane's Addiction** (1991)

"Someone's gotta be put on a pedestal as sex symbols and it might as well be us."
  – *Ian Brown* of **The Stone Roses** (1989)

"My sexuality was going to be packaged for me, so I did it myself."
  – *Liz Phair* (1994)

"You get used to being a sex god."
  – *Dave Gedge* of **The Wedding Present** (1992)

"I prefer snogging and petting to full sex – it leaves more to the imagination."
  – *Jarvis Cocker* of **Pulp** (1995)

"I've been told that I'm quite good. Hell, I'll give myself a seven."
  – *Blackie Onassis* of **Urge Overkill** (1993)

"I tried to discover bisexual sides of myself, but to no avail. One of my girlfriends is bisexual and I absolutely think she's beautiful, but we attempted a snog once and it just wasn't happening for me at all. So I've decided that I am horrifically heterosexual."
  – *Justine Frischmann* of **Elastica** (1994)

"An ingredient of rock has always been this sexual display, and women have been more and more finding out a way that they can do that. Instead of just being the chick in the spandex with the teased up hair that all the guys want to screw, it's more like, 'Yeah, this is how I'm going to project my sexuality, and these are my desires.'"
  – *Tori Amos* (1997)

"I've learned a lot from porno. Besides, it's fun to watch people fucking."
  – *Joshua Todd* of **Buckcherry** (2001)

"There are 400 million sperm in each ejaculation – and if you look around, take a look at some people, it's kinda hard to imagine that they beat 400 million. It makes one wonder."
  – *Tom Waits* (1999)

"If I was a girl, I'd rather fuck a rock star than a plumber."
  – *Gene Simmons* of **Kiss** (circa 1986)

"I'm often told that people fuck to our record. It makes me feel good — that they're putting it to good use."
  – *Shawn Smith* of **Pigeonhed** (2000)

"There are a whole lot of bullies in music today. A lot of music is made by younger, confused people and they're just putting a face on their bewilderment by being really aggressive."
   – *Art Alexakis* of **Everclear** (2001)

"I don't want to sit around criticizing MTV pop culture, but it's depressing. Limp Bizkit is so depressing!"
   – *Rhett Miller* of **Old 97's** (2001)

"I hope rap-metal dies. It's annoying how you could just throw together some lyrics about alienation, get some really loud guitars, dreadlocks and tattoos, and sell records automatically."
   – *Ben* of **The Benjamins** (2001)

"A lot of the bands who were influenced by us were all of a sudden hip and got a lot of airplay. We didn't want to compete with music that sounds like a weaker version of our own songs."
   – *Chino Moreno* of **The Deftones** (2000)

"At least in the eighties all the metal bands were like, 'Yeah I may look stupid and I wear makeup, but all I want to do is get laid.' And while that stuff was also crap, I would much rather see that than, 'Boy am I tough, and boy are we cool, and boy are we intense.'"
   – *Warren Fitzgerald* of **The Vandals** (2000)

"It's basically angry bubble gum. There's not much dimension to it. Slipknot – those guys have got clown masks on for God's sake! If Barnum & Bailey aren't in town, it's cool, but I want some songs, motherfucker. I want something I can sing. Is that too much to ask for?"
   – *Dave Wyndorf* of **Monster Magnet** (2001)

I turn on the TV and there's this band, tattoos, shirts off... I laugh at first, but then I get kind of sad. People really think this is the alternative. It's a bunch of millionaires pretending to be bad boys, pretending to be pivotal components of youth rebellion."
   – *John Reis* of **Rocket From The Crypt** (2001)

Bono of **U2**

"The problem with voting is no matter who you vote for, the government always gets in."
— *Bono* of **U2** (1995)

"Things are so fucking uptight in The United States. Don't listen to that, don't listen to this. Ah, take care of your own family business besides trying to take care of the world, you ignorant asshole. You can't have an abortion... Oh can't I? Just watch me!"
— *Lori Barbiero* of **Babes In Toyland** (1993)

"I never tackled an issue, social, political or otherwise, unless there was a metaphor in which to dress it up. I was never into writing propaganda or polemic."
— *Sting* (2000)

"I do wish all the Government dead. I wish every single one of them a very painful demise. They're hateful."
— *Miles Hunt* of **The Wonder Stuff** (1994)

"I don't think people are converted to socialism by eye contact with me."
— *Billy Bragg* (1997)

"... [I]t's a lot less entertaining to hear about a yeast infection than the Butthole Surfers."
— *Jeff Pinkus* of **The Butthole Surfers** (1993)

"I don't want anyone who's racist or homophobic or intolerant coming to our shows. They can totally fuck off and I'd personally like to kick their asses."
— *Richard Patrick* of **Filter** (1998)

"I have this kinda naïve idea that the world should be a different place than it is right now, and I'd like to be involved in changing it by trying to understand more and be honest about my understanding."
— *Moby* (1999)

"I've got nothing against people who sing about politics. If that's their bag, fine, but I don't think those people have any effect politically. The bottom line is, people buy records and buy concert tickets to be entertained – and everyone knows that."
   – Frank Black (1993)

"More bands ought to make more points about whatever – child abuse, drugs, Exxon, whatever it is they feel passionate about. If you can organize a way to bang the drum and rally some people together, by all means, go for it."
   – Peter Garrett of **Midnight Oil** (1993)

"We applaud the creation of a bomb whose sole purpose is to destroy all mankind, and we grow up watching our President's brains splattered all over Texas. Times have not become more violent, they've become more televised."
   – Marilyn Manson (1999)

"We're not a political band and we don't want to tell people what to do or what to think. We just want to tell them to think. If they're not happy they should get up and do something, even if turns out that they did the wrong thing.
   – Billie Joe Armstrong of **Green Day** (1997)

"I'm more interested these days in the world of psychedelia than the world of politics [laughs]. When you realize that all governments fail at one time or another, it takes the shine off of democracy and all of its speeches and policies. You realize it's all an empty she-bang."
   – Joe Strummer (2001)

"Nelson Mandela? I think he's a complete fake. Anyone that condoned killing and slaughter and all those things that he went to jail for originally. How can he be a man of peace and wisdom and wonder?"
   – John Lydon of **Public Image Ltd.** (1998)

"If Britney Spears would paint her ass green, I'm sure you could spot green asses all over L.A. as soon as the word was out."
  – *Billie Joe Armstrong* of **Green Day** (2000)

"I just figured out how to say Mariah. You say it like pariah."
  – *Michael Stipe* of **R.E.M.** (1991)

"I've done a Debbie Gibson song when she was big. The Fellows did 'Shake Your Love." I like that song, I wouldn't have done it otherwise."
  – *Scott McCaughey* of **The Young Fresh Fellows**
     and **The Minus 5** (2001)

"I like seeing our records go up and Kylie and Phil Collins go down. There's no point moaning about it, you've got to get in there and stamp them out."
  – *Ian Brown* of **The Stone Roses** (1990)

"I don't think the Backstreet Boys would wanna hang out with us."
  – *Robert Sledge* of **The Ben Folds Five** (1999)

"I love a good dance ditty. God, I love disco. I see no problem admiring the Bee Gees and being in The Sex Pistols."
  – *Johnny "Rotten" Lydon* (1998)

"Britney Spears wears a school suit too. She looks cuter in it than me, I'll give her that. It's when she starts playing guitar, that's when I'll start to worry, I think."
  – *Angus Young* of **AC/DC** (2000)

"I think popular music sucks today. For the most part, I cannot fucking stand the shit that's at the top of the charts. Now, I'm not saying my sole mission is to turn people on to other music. But maybe I can change things a bit."
  – *Trent Reznor* of **Nine Inch Nails** (1996)

Fred Durst of **Limp Bizkit**

Photo by Rahav Segev/Photopass.com

"Nirvana were one of the only bands that were in the same ballpark as us nihilistically, aesthetically and spiritually."

    – *Curt Kirkwood* of the **Meat Puppets** (1994)

"I have a lot of respect for Tom Morello [of Rage Against The Machine], not just for how he plays but also for his head. He's not just an inventive guitarist, he's also a smart guy. It's nice to hear his interviews. He's not some L.A. 'I wanna be a rock star' bonehead. There should be more people that aware and accountable."

    – *Kim Thayil* of **Soundgarden** (1999)

"It's great to look at Green Day, selling millions of records to kids like my little brother, it's great that he's listening to that instead of, say, Poison."

    – *Bill Janovitz* of **Buffalo Tom** (1995)

"I never met Johnny Rotten, but I like what he did to people."

    – *Neil Young* (circa 1989)

"The Sex Pistols got it right, man; they made a good record, then blew up. I love that."

    – *Chris Ballew* of **The Presidents of the United States of America** (2000)

"I think Fugazi is one of the only bands around that I would say are punk both musically and idealistically. You just can't find anyone in the music business who is as true to what they believe as Ian MacKaye."

    – *Tom Daily,* ex-**Smoking Popes**

"Bad Religion was unlike anything I had ever seen. So much fucking energy. So loud! So fast! I remember Greg Graffin saluting all of the crowd surfers. There was mass chaos in the crowd – sweat and ten-hole Doc Marten boots. Some kid came over with a bloody nose. As we stumbled back to our car after the show, I kept thinking, 'Holy shit. What the fuck was that?'"

    – *Mark Hoppus* of **Blink 182** (2001)

"A band like Blink 182, I think they totally have the same kind of irreverent attitude and the same ability to have fun with punk that bands like the Dickies had back in 1979."
  – *Dexter Holland* of **The Offspring** (2001)

"Tom Waits, man. Him and Eminem and Bob Dylan. That's the big three. You can't argue with them."
  – *Chris Martin* of **Coldplay** (2000)

"I met Coldplay, and they were nice guys. But then I heard 'Yellow' and thought, 'Oh, that's a big song. That's a huge song.'"
  – *Fran Healy* of **Travis** (2001)

"Van Morrison has been so much a part of my life, since I was a kid in school. It's a thrill to hear him singing a song I've written, because of what Van's music has meant to me over the years. I hope we can do some more."
  – *Mark Knopfler,* ex-**Dire Straits** (2000)

"Gordon Lightfoot, we love him. He's great. We love all that stuff. Roberta Flack too. A lot of it is good for sampling."
  – *Jill Cunniff* of **Luscious Jackson** (1996)

"Chrissie Hynde said our record was the best thing she's heard in ten years. We were amazed. I mean, this is someone who was part of the reason we all picked up guitars in the first place."
  – *Eddie "King" Roesner* of **Urge Overkill** (1993)

"Dylan is a rare performer – he has a sense of what it takes to allow that spontaneity to happen. Neil Young and Van Morrison have it too; they know how to allow that conscious moment to happen. It's that magic which keeps them so intriguing.
  – *Mike Scott* of **The Waterboys** (2000)

"Nick Drake was fucked up, a one-take kind of artist: walked in, played the songs, walked out. Completely brilliant."
    – *Courtney Taylor* of **The Dandy Warhols** (2000)

"Frank Sinatra is the coolest dude that ever walked the planet. Followed closely by Lou Reed, Leonard Cohen... Jim Morrison was cool, but he was a bit of a dullard. And, of course, there was me, and that's about it, really."
    – *Ian McCulloch* of **Echo & The Bunnymen** (1992)

Bob Pollard of **Guided By Voices**   Photo by Jason Homa

"I had black hair so people said we were goth. Now I have red hair so people say we're glam."
   – *Marilyn Manson* (1998)

"People think we are supposed to be the leaders of some sort of 'gloom movement.'"
   – *Robert Smith* of **The Cure** (1992)

"I think musicians are seduced into believing that you have to pledge allegiance to a point of view and a style and a dress code."
   – *Joe Henry* (2001)

"You've gotta feel sorry for kids these days. They really don't have anything to listen to. When we were kids, we bought our records based on what we heard on the radio, and the stuff was good. It was song-oriented, you know? Now, everything is image and technology-oriented."
   – *Bob Pollard* of **Guided By Voices** (2001)

"What we look like shouldn't matter. We're a fucking fantastic band for ordinary people."
   – *Fran Healy* of **Travis** (2001)

"It's my life and my body, and if I want to fuck myself up and have a beard and wear my hair long, that's my business."
   – *Elvis Costello* (1991)

"I don't really like it when I learn about new bands from their ads in magazines. I want to hear something about them by word of mouth first."
   – *Matt Murphy* of **The Flashing Lights** (2000)

"While we had a reputation as rampaging sexual vandals, the truth is that most of the time we were looking for nothing at bedtime other than a good paperback."
   – *Robert Plant* (1985), ex-**Led Zeppelin**

"The socks on our dicks, the way we jump around onstage, all that shit has always been a natural extension of the music."
   – *Flea* of **The Red Hot Chili Peppers** (1995)

"I kind of hate that I'm being called the waif. All of a sudden I'm, like, skinny rich bitch, and this is fucking hilariously terrible. I have the public image of the exact person that I've fought against for my entire life. If it weren't partly my fault, then it wouldn't be happening."
   – *Fiona Apple* (1997)

"I've loved this kind of music for twenty years. When I first got into it, sterilized, over-produced arena rock was the mainstream and you got beat up for liking punk."
  – *Noodles* of **The Offspring** (2000)

"The whole idea of punk, which I came out of, was that you didn't have to be able to play. And I couldn't. That was the charm and the joy of it."
  – *Robert Smith* of **The Cure** (1996)

"The Police liked the energy of punk, but we couldn't really be a part of it. One of our problems was we were quite good at playing our instruments – that was definitely a handicap. You were supposed to have just come in off the streets, having never played a bass or sang before."
  – *Sting* (circa 1993)

"Punk rock, which used to involve taking shit and physical confronta-tions for granted, like one takes for granted a favorite pair of Pro Keds, has come to mean fitting in, not rocking the boat, paying lip service to pop cultural icons and ideas and, above all, maintaining an affected disinterest in the society which props it up from behind."
  – *Steve Albini* of **Big Black** (1985)

"When I got into it, being a punk was almost a decision to remove yourself from society. You were a loner at school and you probably wound up getting in fights everyday. That's what I had to put up with. Now, although the ideals are there, you can be different. In high school there's a whole table of punk kids at lunchtime to sit with."
  – *Joe Escalante* of **The Vandals** (2000)

"When I read about the new punk explosion, I just thought it was so fucking stupid. Now it's happening to me, and it's still pretty fucking stupid."
  – *Billie Joe Armstrong* of **Green Day** (1994)

"The whole nihilism thing of punk meant nothing to me."
   – *Paul Weller,* formerly of **The Jam** (1995)

"While you have gallons of Mohawks and leather jackets telling you that they do what they want, I don't believe them. I respect the person that says, 'I don't care for that' because there is no extreme, it's pure sincerity. Punk is doing what you want despite the infiltrators, outside of the skateboards and shoes and hair and patches and the diets and the tattoos.
   – *Devon Williams* of **Osker** (2001)

"I was raised in Navy housing by the government. Punk rock was a way to get out and pursue the pioneer thing – to make your own road, build your own house, be intense, and get together with other dudes with intense ideas."
   – *Mike Watt* of **fIREHOSE** (1995)

"I'm punk rock everyday. It comes from my background. I got into punk to survive. My dad was an alcoholic, a total drunk. I could go into my room, listen to punk and shut the world out. It was the safest place I could find."
   – *Tim Armstrong* of **Rancid** (1995)

"Punk was being the only one with short hair in your high school, being beaten up by Boston fans calling you 'Devo.'"
   – *Dr. Frank* of **The Mr. T Experience** (2001)

"In punk, I think the word 'sellout' is thrown around way too lightly. People are just looking for you to do anything that doesn't suit them and then you're a sellout in their eyes, so, I don't give too much credence to that. Basically, as a band, we try to do what we think is right artistically, and in business, and in mind. But you really can't make a dollar without someone somewhere deeming you to be a sellout. We just try to stay true to ourselves."
   – *Trevor Keith* of **Face To Face** (2000)

"Mostly, punk was funny. We couldn't believe we were getting away with it."
   – *Pete Shelley* of **The Buzzcocks** (2001)

"What I wanted to do was approach the music with the same attitude, the same attack as punk, without sacrificing all of the things I liked about music. As a result, I had a goody-goody image to a lot of people."
   – *Elvis Costello* (1994)

"The whole gist of original punk was to annoy, outrage and shock people."
   – *Larry Livermore* of Lookout Records (1995)

"Being punk rock is not having to prove you are. It's obvious to anyone who is authentic in that mindset. You don't have to call yourself a punk rocker."
   – *Thurston Moore* of **Sonic Youth** (1994)

"Musicians who didn't pay attention to punk have a gap in their knowledge that makes it difficult to communicate in this day and age."
   – *Flea* of **The Red Hot Chili Peppers** (1992)

"Punk will always be punk. There will always be a subculture whose anthem is bouncing off a basement wall."
   – *Dan Didier* of **The Promise Ring** (2001)

"When I was a teenager in the Valley, taking black beauties and going to see Black Flag, being a punk rocker was like taking a vow of unpopularity. And the records were hard to find."
   – *Brett Gurewitz* of Epitaph Records (1995)

"There seems to be a cycle every few years, where the music becomes bloated and something comes along to strip it down. The Sex Pistols did it to stadium rock and Nirvana did it to the hair bands. Who knows, maybe punk rock – like Green Day, like Pennywise, like us – will do it to Seattle."
   – *Dexter Holland* of **The Offspring** (1994)

"Joe Strummer and I must have been the first punks they'd ever seen in Jamaica — we had our zippers and our leather jackets and all that — they must've thought we were Martians."
   — *Mick Jones,* ex-**The Clash** and **Big Audio Dynamite** (1994)

"The people who think we're just copying the old punks are guys driving BMWs with anarchy stickers on their bumpers."
   — *Lars Frederiksen* of **Rancid** (1995)

"One of the great things about punk is that it discouraged people from getting jobs. It gave me and other people the inspiration not to be forced into a soul-destroying job, but to get money in other ways."
   — *Bobby Gillespie* of **Primal Scream** (1991)

"It just won't die! Southern California seems to be a breeding ground. That word of mouth is coming from older brothers and older sisters or, God forbid, moms and dads who have teenage kids now."
   — *Mike Ness* of **Social Distortion** (1996)

"I hated most of the punk bands. There was only the Pistols and the Clash that I really liked. I thought the rest were fucking rubbish. It's all right getting all dewy-eyed and nostalgic, but it was fucking awful."
   — *Paul Weller,* ex-**The Jam** (1994)

"The only point I could make about the Pistols, being an eyewitness, is that they could absolutely play. The four of them could get on a shite stage on a shite Tuesday night, and the sound you'd hear was total."
   — *Joe Strummer,* ex-**The Clash** (2001)

"We weren't really a punk group. We were doing stuff that was weird for punk people. One of the first things I remember is playing to an audience in Liverpool where they were literally standing in a semi-circle against the wall: They were crowded as far away from us and they could, like they were petrified of us."
   — *Colin Newman* of **Wire** (2000)

"It wasn't like, 'These guys are great!' the thought was, 'Fuckin' A! If these wankers can make music, we can make music.' Thing was, The Sex Pistols were funny. Punks knew they looked ridiculous."
   – *Bernard Sumner* of **New Order** (1993)

"It's only recently that punk rock underground music took on one more eccentric tentacle – that to be a really bitchin' punk rock band you must also be successful. I don't know how that happened, since the very word underground means that your style and substance and art should preempt your actual commercial endeavor."
   – *Curt Kirkwood* of **The Meat Puppets** (1994)

"Everyone thinks the British started punk, but we did when we started in '74. When we played London in 1977, people like Johnny Rotten, The Clash and The Damned all told us we were responsible."
   – *Joey Ramon*e (1993)

"Nobody's gonna like you guys, but I'll have you back."
   – *Hilly Kristal,* owner of CBGB, to the Ramones
      after their first audition (1974)

Mike Ness of **Social Distortion**   Photo by Jason Homa

"I was a real bad drinker and really bad with the speed. When I got out of that whole routine, I was 25, and I said, 'It's time to stop this shit because I'm not going to make it to 30 if I keep it up.'"
  – *Bob Mould,* of **Sugar,** ex-**Husker Du** (1993)

"I quit drugs before I quit drinking because drugs were taking their toll on me. I was sick of the headaches and the puking and the shitting blood. I figured I'd stop everything but alcohol, but then I overcompensated with drinking."
  – *Lars Frederiksen* of **Rancid** (1995)

"When I shot junk, you could go to jail for a long time and now they just send you to rehab and the record company pays."
  – *Iggy Pop* (1995)

"Take the drugs away and there's more time for sex and rock & roll."
  – *Steven Tyler* of **Aerosmith** (1987)

"I was racing head first toward destruction. I had no intention of getting myself better. I thought I was a drug addict and I was going to die a drug addict and I thought I had a couple of years to live at best. I had a couple of ODs and near death experiences. I knew I was dead meat, so I made the choice and decided to get clean. After that I miraculously started making friends again. I was such a monster."
  – *Brett Gurewitz,* founder of Epitaph Records (1996)

"Drug treatment is a unique experience somewhat akin to chemotherapy. I'd recommend it to anyone."
  – *Mark Lanegan* of **The Screaming Trees** (1998)

"The fun thing about being sober is meeting all the friends I've had for years, especially the ones I've never met."
  – *Alice Cooper* (circa 1990)

"I knew I needed to be sober for years. But I didn't want it enough."
  – *Scott Weiland* of **Stone Temple Pilots** (2000)

Courtney Love of **Hole**   Photo by Rahav Segev/Photopass.com

"Rock 'n roll is like a drug. I don't take very much, but when I do rock 'n roll, I fuckin' do it. But I don't want to do it all the time 'cause it'll kill me."
— *Neil Young* (1988)

"Rock & roll doesn't have a soul, only a dick and a wallet."
— *Kim Thayil* of **Soundgarden** (1994)

"I never thought of rock & roll as this big cultural thing and worried about the state of it and all. It's like, plug that fucking guitar in and give me a backbeat, and 'it' lives."
— *Paul Westerberg,* ex-**The Replacements** (1993)

"I like some of the showmanship and gimmicks of rock & roll, whether it's Chuck Berry's duck walk, Pete Townshend's flailing arms, or the Sex Pistols anti-promotion."
— *Peter Gabriel* (1986)

"I made rock my religion, that was my church. I said, 'I love it so much, and I can't get enough of it, so I need to write. I need to add to it, and write more."
— *Bob Pollard* of **Guided By Voices** (2001)

"Rock & roll is about attitude. I couldn't care less about technique."
— *Johnny Thunders* (1977)

"For me, rock & roll is all about when you're in a bar and you're in love with someone and you want to fuck them and a band's playing."
— *Mark Eitzel* of **American Music Club** (1994)

"There is no clandestine value to rock'n'roll music. No excitement. It's totally unrevolutionary. It's totally accepted and part of everything. It's totally pushed."
— *Debbie Harry* of **Blondie** (circa 1981)

"Rock & roll is not so much a question of electric guitars as it is striped pants."
  – *David Lee Roth* (circa 1985)

"Rock & roll is the lowest form of life known to man."
  – *Elvis Costello* (1977)

"One chord is fine. Two chords are pushing it. Three chords and you're into jazz."
  – *Lou Reed* (circa 1975)

"I guess it's all just music the way I look at it. It's hard to call it rock & roll anymore…I think rock & roll is dead."
  – *Billie Joe Armstrong* of **Green Day** (1995)

"Rock music can't teach us anything we don't already know."
  – *Stephen Malkmus* of **Pavement** (1997)

"I think I'm less about rock & roll and more about songs. I could live without rock & roll. I haven't got this sort of religious reverie for rock & roll. I think it's incredibly reactionary and boring."
  – *Sting* (1993)

"I don't listen to rock music. I don't listen to any white music."
  – *Ian Brown* of **The Stone Roses** (1994)

"I know nothing about rock & roll. Do you know, until recently I thought that Led Zeppelin sang 'Smoke On The Water?'"
  – *Justine Frischmann* of **Elastica** (1994)

"I do think rock & roll should be glamorous and beautiful and sexy."
  – *Tanya Donnelly* of **Belly** (1995)

"Rock & roll is an expression of the energy of life, the energy that comes from the realization you're alive, projecting it outwards. You just wanna stamp your feet and wave your hands in the air."
  – *Ian Astbury* of The Cult (2001)

"When you listen to good rock & roll you wanna feel fucking dirty afterwards. You should feel so dirty you have to take a shower. Rock & roll should be like pornography...The filthier the better."
 – *Frank Black* (1996)

"The best rock & roll music encapsulates a certain high energy – an angriness – whether on record or onstage. Rock & roll is only rock & roll if it's not safe."
 – *Mick Jagger* of **The Rolling Stones** (circa 1981)

"Sex and drugs and rock & roll, that's what I think is wrong with rock & roll."
 – *Kim Thayil* of **Soundgarden** (1992)

"I don't like rock & roll bullshit. I like to give people a show. I like to give people their money's worth. But I don't like putting a foot on the monitor, playing a guitar solo, and begging to be worshipped."
 – *John Reis* of **Rocket From The Crypt** (2001)

"As much as I'd like to say we're about the destruction of rock music, our culture is rock culture. When I was a kid, my life was about going home and lip-syncing to Thin Lizzy records."
 – *M. Doughty* of **Soul Coughing** (1998)

Ray Davies of **The Kinks**   Photo by Jason Homa

"Our audience doesn't come to see theatrics… they realize we're not performers, and that we're a group that's earnestly trying to accomplish something, and we don't quite know what it is."
  – *Jerry Garcia* of **The Grateful Dead** (circa 1987)

"Onstage, I've been hit by a grapefruit, beer cans, eggs, spit, money, cigarette butts, mandies, Quaaludes, joints, bras, panties and a fist."
  – *Iggy Pop* (1986)

"I think it's kind of neat when you get 5,000 people singing in unison, "I'm not a trendy asshole."
  – *Noodles* of **The Offspring** (1997)

"I don't know where I am when I'm singing. I don't take care of my voice when I'm performing. I just lose my head. I'm gone."
  – *Adam Duritz* of **The Counting Crows** (1996)

"The whole idea of being a DJ is working a club and making people do things, making people enjoy themselves or feel something."
  – *Tom Rowlands* of **The Chemical Brothers** (1999)

"When I'm onstage, I'm just in this floating energy field – it's hard to explain. I have a really addictive personality; that's why I don't fuck with cocaine or shit like that. If I did, I think I'd just get lost in it. So I've found my true addiction: rockin' a show."
  – *Coby Dick* of **Papa Roach** (2000)

"I've never ever heard two thousand people in unison shout 'fuck off!' I say, 'we can't really go on 'cos there's a curfew here' and two thousand people went 'fuck off!' simultaneously, yet all together. Then I went back to the band and said 'sorry lads, we're not finished yet!'
  – *Joe Strummer,* on performing with his
    band **The Mescaleros** (2000)

"People lose themselves at the show - they think they're watching a movie. They forget it's me up there. The good thing is that I forget it's me as well."
    – *Ray Davies* of **The Kinks** (1998)

"I love to hear the crowd sing along. I get the biggest hard-on from that. Of course, it means I have an erection for a whole hour every night."
    – *Chester Bennington* of **Linkin Park** (2001)

"Performing is the glorious release. The point of the tour is that the only life you have is the hour that you're onstage. It's the essential focus of it all, the whole essence. Everything is waiting for that. Your life is dependent on that one hour."
    – *David Thomas* of **Pere Ubu** (circa 1988)

"When I'm on the stage, I'm not in control of myself at all. I don't even know who I am. I'm not this rational person who can sit here now and talk to you. If you walked on the stage with a microphone in the middle of the concert, I'd probably come close to killing you."
    – *Pete Townshend* (1982)

"Rock & roll is the only job where you show up for work, and there's four cases of beer, a bottle of vodka and a bottle of tequila at your desk."
  – *Mark McGrath* of **Sugar Ray** (2001)

"Mark chooses to live the lifestyle. He parties every single night of the week. He's the most Hollywood guy of all time. He's gotta be seen."
  – *DJ Homicide* of **Sugar Ray** on bandmate
    Mark McGrath (2001)

"I'm trying to lead the life of a rock & roll star. There's a lot you have to know. You have to learn how to do all sorts of crazy things, like wake up in the morning with a bottle of Jack Daniels in your hand."
  – *John McDermott* of **Stroke 9** (1999)

"The wildest rock & roll thing I've ever done was when I threw my guitar into the audience one time and cracked a guy's head open. That was pretty wild."
  – *J Mascis* of **Dinosaur Jr.** (1993)

"People encourage rock stars to act like children. You can act like a big spoiled baby and think it's great."
  – *Noel Gallagher* of **Oasis** (1995)

"Rock star means, like rich asshole. That's a 1980's thing. No matter what anyone says, I'm too deeply rooted to just turn asshole over night."
  – *Mike Dirnt* of **Green Day** (1995)

"You've got to look at the context in which I'm operating. I'm in a traveling rock band. I wear leather pants. I get a certain number of people who are looking for a certain experience, and I'm the designated guy."
  – *Dave Wyndorf* of **Monster Magnet** (2001)

"Not to seem crass, but I've been trying to be a rock star for years, so I only hang out with rock stars. I'll only date rock stars, hot bods or royal titles."
  – *Rufus Wainwright* (2001)

"You know, we were trying to be rock stars for years, and so far it hasn't really clicked for us."
  – *Donald Fagen* of **Steely Dan** (2001)

"I would think nothing of tipping over a table with a long spread on it just because there was turkey roll on the table and I had said, 'No turkey roll.'"
  – *Steven Tyler* of **Aerosmith** (2001)

"My job is to wear make-up, stick out my tongue and try to fuck everything that moves within a thousand-yard radius of the stage."
  – *Gene Simmons* of **Kiss** (1999)

"I recommend to anyone who wants to be a rock star, if that doesn't pan out, become a cook."
  – *Chris Cornell* of **Soundgarden** (1992)

"If I had my way I would have sex, drugs and rock & roll at least four to six hours a day."
  – *Perry Farrell* of **Jane's Addiction** (circa 1993)

"Rock & roll seems like a fun thing to do. You get to sleep late and hang out with all your friends, drink beer and listen to the music that you like. It's not always as much fun as people think it is. I guess I just lucked out that I like writing songs and people like my songs. That's the catch. You do what you like and that's fine, but if no one else likes it, eventually, you run out of steam."
  – *Wayne Coyne* of **The Flaming Lips** (1999)

"We embrace the rock & roll lifestyle, since it's all we do. Of course we exaggerate in our lyrics to make them funnier, but we like to party."
  – *Maya Ford* of **The Donnas** (2001)

"Sometimes a woman can really persuade you to make an asshole of yourself."
  – *Rod Stewart* (2001)

"Rock & roll wives... I hate 'em."
  – *Mick Jagger* of **The Rolling Stones** (circa 1976)

"Today's woman puts on wigs, fake eyelashes, false fingernails, sixteen pounds of assorted make-up/shadows/blushes/creams, living bras, various pads that would make a linebacker envious, has implants and assorted other surgeries, then complains that she cannot find a "real" man."
  – *Maynard James Keenan* of **Tool** (1996)

"We happen to be feminists but that's not the basis of the band. I think any woman who is in the work place is lying to herself if she doesn't call herself a feminist. It's kind of like a black person saying they're not into black power."
  – *Donita Sparks* of **L7** (1994)

"When I first started to get out there, people thought: militant, angry, man-hating, puppy-eating feminist. Yikes! Now it's different. There's the industry hype of chick singers in rock, plus a lot of female-informed rock out there. People are getting more used to the idea of the girl with the big mouth."
  – *Ani Difranco* (1994)

"'Girl' is not menstruating, 'Girl' is non-orgasmic, 'Girl' is naïve, cute, bratty, unthreatening in her clumsiness and incompetence. 'Girl' is, most of all, young. It is vanity in extremes. I have always called myself a girl, but I am going to stop now."
  –*Courtney Love* of **Hole** (1994)

"In the larger context of feminism and hatred against women, sex discrimination at rock shows is just another strategy meant to keep us at home. It's meant to keep public space male, and to keep us feeling afraid."
   – *Kathleen Hanna* of **Bikini Kill** (2000)

"When I started, I got a lot of attention because I was aggressive, strident. People liked that."
   – *Shirley Manson* of **Garbage** (1999)

"Feminists should be concerned about the personalities in rock & roll because they will be the primary means by which young women get the feminist message."
   – **Camille Paglia**, controversial cultural critic (1995)

"They run and leap into the audience. I wish it had been like that when I was younger. There are a lot more girls going to gigs. They're at the front, not at the back with their boyfriend. The front."
   – *Saffron* of **Republica** (1996)

"At first, feminism conjured up these pictures – bra-burning, that sort of thing. As more time went on, I started to understand what feminism was. It's just the right of equality professionally and personally and politically. It's so reasonable."
   – *Melissa Etheridge* (1997)

"Men would prefer to ignore women's complications, because it's a natural instinct to ignore any complications that aren't your own. For women that grew up male-fixated, it's long been appealing to keep it to yourself and make sure honey's happy."
   – *Liz Phair* (1994)

"I think that people get into relationships for the wrong reasons. I think that people look to their partners to make themselves complete. They lean on people too much. They drain their partners of their energy. The only kinds of relationships that work, and work

forever, are the kind between two complete independent people. I think that too many relationships are about weird psychoses."
  – *Fiona Apple* (1997)

"Listen, the easiest way to get laid by a girl, or get rid of her, is to write a song about her."
  – *David Crosby* (1970s)

"When I meet a woman, I don't think, 'Gee, I wonder if she's read the latest thesis by Stephen Hawking? I think, 'Great Tits!'"
  – *Gene Simmons* of **Kiss** (1996)

"The whole cliché of women being cathartic really pisses me off. You know, 'Oh, this is therapy for me. I'd die if I didn't write this.' Eddie Vedder says shit like that. Fuck you."
  – *Courtney Love* of **Hole** (1994)

"I'm gonna bring me a bitch back tonight. In fact, I'm gonna bring me three bitches back tonight."
  – *Eminem* (1999)

"What would make a young woman today think that taking off her shirt at a concert is a good idea? Everything would make you think that. Everything! The world tells you that. Look anywhere! Watch VH-1's "Behind The Music," the Def Leppard one, where girls were pulling up their shirts in the crowd and the band would, like, pick the one they wanted."
  – *Kathleen Hanna* of **Bikini Kill** (2000)

Moby

Photo by Dominic Episcopo

"There should be a government scheme to encourage people to make music. The way things work in a band is not like any other job. You have to be ready before you can earn any wages – how can you get ready if you are going to have to graft six days a week?"
   – *Richard Ashcroft* of **The Verve** (1998)

"What was totally unacceptable and immoral ten years ago is mild and totally acceptable today. The state of society, where the line of morality is concerned, is not only being sold to us in copious amounts of propaganda and advertising, but is constantly moving."
   – *Jason Miller* of **Godhead** (2000)

"If you don't confront censorship, then the music of confrontational artists will be silenced."
   – *Tom Morello* of Rage Against The Machine (1993)

"Censorship is the most stupid thing in this country. I find Americans should liberate – go through a positive kind of development. That's what I pray for. I say 'fuck' and 'shit' whenever I please."
   – *Sasha Konietzko* of **KMFDM** (1995)

"For a long time people could see the world very simply. There was a Soviet influence and there was the Western influence. And now that's been broken down and a lot of cultures are up for grabs I think people find themselves reverting to not particularly challenging cultural standards. People don't want culture to challenge them anymore."
   – *Moby* (1997)

"I was never to blame for Columbine and I think people realize that now. Events like that have happened for years before my time, before all of our time, and I think the important thing that should be learned from that is that a lot of young people growing up are pissed off because no one's listening to what they're saying. So sometimes they have to say things in an ugly way and it should be a reminder to listen to what your kids are saying."
   – *Marilyn Manson* (2000)

R.E.M.

Photo by Jason Homa

"There's always going to be the bands who change the way the river flows, and there are always going to be people who get in their boats and ride down afterwards."
   – *Billy Corgan* of **Smashing Pumpkins** (1993)

"I used to have almost a sickness about big dumb rock. Now I'm realizing that it's a force that can be used for good or evil."
   – *John McCrea* of **Cake** (2001)

"Artists everywhere steal mercilessly all the time and I think this is healthy."
   – *Peter Gabriel* (1992)

"I feel like my generation was the last generation that had expectations, and then shit didn't pan out. Everybody is so fucking bitter. When it got hard, they all fucking gave up. And they're just bitter assholes now."
   – *David Lowery* of **Cracker** (1996)

"Making music is like having loads of kids. I've got hundreds and hundreds of babies out there in people's homes, on their shelves. Little bits of me, all around the world."
   – *Richard James* of **Aphex Twin** (1998)

"Groups with guitars are on the way out."
   – A Decca Records executive canceling a 1961 *Beatles* audition

"I'm just bursting on the scene like a pathetic, gold-plated sperm."
   – *Beck* (1994)

"Good taste stifles creativity."
   – *Perry Farrell* of **Jane's Addiction** (1990)

"Going to a 7-Eleven in the middle of the night and hearing the clerk whistling one of my songs – that's my idea of a great cover version."
   – *Warren Zevon* (2000)

"Just because the songs are about reality, there's no reason for music to be boring or depressing. Music is about uplifting people, you know?"
— *Shane MacGowan,* ex-**Pogues** (1995)

"The majority of pop stars are complete idiots in every respect."
— *Sade* (2000)

"You can communicate more with a scream over feedback than most college professors can in an entire dissertation."
— *Zack De La Rocha* of **Rage Against The Machine** (1999)

"Anybody that forms a group, writes songs and releases records and says they don't care if people like them are complete liars."
— *James Dean Bradfield* of the **Manic Street Preachers** (2001)

"You've got to be able to hold a lot of contradictory ideas in your mind without going nuts. I feel like to do my job right, when I walk out onstage I've got to feel like it's the most important thing in the world. I've also got to feel like, well, it's only rock & roll. Somehow you've got to believe both of those things."
— *Bruce Springsteen* (2000)

"In any band there's two camps: the lead singer's camp and the guitarist's camp. The guitar player you work with; it's like riding a fuckin' horse. He's gonna buck — that's his job. He wants to dominate you and scare you so they can dominate the band. Ron (Asheton) and James (Williamson) were like that — they wanted control. Any guitar player worth his salt is basically a thug."
— *Iggy Pop* (1999)

"I think music was more important, more capable of effecting a change in people's attitudes, when it was less accessible. 'Cause it's like drugs then, people want it 'cause they can't get it."
— *Elvis Costello* (1989)

"In two centuries' time, people are going to look at the music of this age and see Goldie and The Beach Boys as working at the same time. Twenty years isn't going to make much difference. Most people won't even know what came first, The Beatles or drum 'n' bass."
    – *Jean-Benoit Dunckel* of **Air** (2000)

"It's not like some band set out to be innovative and they were. It's not really this kind of genius vision or anything. It was like, how do we make something out of this little pile of chord progressions and slightly pretentious college-dropout poetry and impress people down at the Rathskellar?"
    – *Frank Black* (2001)

"Every five years it seems like people start proclaiming that rock is dead 'cause there's something new that comes along. It never is."
    – *David Lowery* of **Cracker** (1998)

"Art is born inside someone and comes out into something that you can experience and that's all it is. There's no difference between Beethoven and Johnny Rotten. There's no difference between Beethoven and me."
    – *Adam Duritz* of **Counting Crows** (1998)

"If you look at the history of innovation in music, it all happens by accident. Innovative music has never come, from my perspective, from a bunch of academics sitting around."
    – *Moby* (2001)

"It's really easy for a singer to destroy a great song. That's why I don't like to see myself as a singer but rather an instrument within the band, the fifth instrument in a great band. A voice should blend in and complete the sound of a band and not destroy it. I have seen and heard that with too many other bands and I want to avoid it all costs."
    – *Chino Moreno* of **The Deftones** (2000)

"When something that's considered secret and wonderful is revealed to the world, it becomes a little less wonderful. It's time to find something new; that's a legitimate and healthy cycle."
  – *Michael Stipe* of **R.E.M.** (2001)

"Guitar players are, for the most part, worthless creatures, but at least they make the strings vibrate."
  – *Stephen Malkmus* of **Pavement** (1994)

"The guitar's pretty phallic. The mics are pretty phallic. It's all from that place. It's all from man's sexual area. But in a lot of ways it's what men have been doing for thousands of years, you know, they're beating on drums to get the girls to come out of their houses and look at them. 'Come out and look at me. We're all dressed up, we're all colorful. Take the best.'"
  – *Ian Astbury* of **The Cult** (2001)

"Guitars don't grow in a field or on trees. The only form of musical expression that's not artificial is either singing or banging on your body."
  – *Moby,* in defense of electronic music (2001)

"I'm into black radio, but they're not into me."
  – *Lenny Kravitz* (1993)

"There's been a serious lack of cool dudes to fall in love with in rock in the last few years."

    – Ruyter Suys of **Nashville Pussy** (2000)

"Today music has become really clean and the messages being pumped across are sterile, played-out messages. Nobody is really saying what is going on in their lives; it's all bloody shiny cars and beautiful girls. Now, I love beautiful girls, but it is all about fantasy, it's not really part of my life."

    – Rob Birch of **Stereo MC's** (2001)

"The strict formatting isn't good for the future of music. Everything's been airbrushed down into the same thing. It's stagnating. But, it is good in the sense that it drives everything back to the underground, which is where good music always was. It gives it back to the hipsters who are willing to go searching for things."

    – Joe Strummer (2001)

"Mainstream rock radio is defiantly very Denny's-like, McDonald's even. It's kind of bland, kind of greasy, kind of not very good… not very high quality."

    – Frank Black (2001)

"You shouldn't have to worry about where you come from. We just want to get good music back on the charts."

    – Chris Martin of **Coldplay** (2001)

"The state of rock today definitely hurts our chances of getting to a wider audience. As far as having any commercial potential, now is the best time for us, except the music out there now just jive. But eventually something might happen again. Things go in cycles."

    – Bob Pollard of **Guided By Voices** (2001)

"There's this perspective out there that audiences don't need depth, they just need fodder. I don't think that at all."

    – Dave Matthews (2001)

Shirley Manson of **Garbage**   Photo by Rahav Segev/Photopass.com

"It's hardly Paul McCartney leaving The Beatles."
- **Noel Gallagher**, on Bonehead's departure from **Oasis** (1999)

"I saw the birth of Britpop and it was horrible."
- **Phil** of **Lo-Fidelity Allstars** (1999)

"Look where Johnny Rotten is now. Fat and wearing bad clothing."
- **Perry Farrell** of **Jane's Addiction** (1996)

"After meeting Bono, it made me want to give up being in a rock & roll band."
- **Dave Grohl** of **Nirvana** (1992)

"I think English art is rubbish. I think English groups are rubbish. I think English books are rubbish and I think English films are rubbish."
- **Mark E. Smith** of **The Fall** (1998)

"Fuck 'NSYNC, Fuck Backstreet Boys, Fuck Britney Spears, Fuck Christina Aguilera, fuck all that bullshit. That shit is trash to me, fucking no talent."
- **Eminem** (2000)

"That was Courtney's downfall - she tried to compete with me and she lost."
- **Marilyn Manson** (1999)

"All these other bands around are just so boring it makes me sick. Fuck them all. I hope they die."
- **Bobby Gillespie** of **Primal Scream** (2000)

"Classic Van Halen made you want to drink, dance and fuck. Current Van Halen encourages us to drink milk, drive a Nissan and have a relationship."
- **David Lee Roth** (1996)

"Who gives a shit what people say? It's spew. It's their vomit."
- **Curt Kirkwood** of **The Meat Puppets** (1994)

"I'm resigning for medical reasons: Billy Corgan makes me sick."
  – *Sharon Osbourne* (2000), ex-**Smashing Pumpkins** manager

"I went to law school for three years – three miserable years – with the worst scum of the earth: children of the affluent families during the height of the Reagan Revolution. It was hell. Just imagine stepping into a sea of pricks every day."
  – *Santiago Durango* of **Big Black** (2000)

"The only good thing about the Spice Girls is that you can look at them with the sound turned down."
  – *George Harrison* (1999)

"I just wish Eddie Vedder would get on with it and kill himself."
  – *Noel Gallagher* of **Oasis** (1996)

"It wasn't always comfortable competing against Nirvana, and it was certainly not healthy living under that shadow at times. But at least there was honor in it. We all respected that it was a great band – Pearl Jam too. But competing against Bush? It's nothing to get your dick hard about, you know what I mean? There's no mojo in that!"
  – *Billy Corgan* of **Smashing Pumpkins** (1996)

"Sid Vicious was just a mindless twerp. I didn't find anything at all romantic about him – or even interesting."
  – *David Bowie* (circa 1983)

"I fucking hate college students to tell you the truth, because they've been able to go to school, get an education, live in the dorms, and get a free ride from their parents. I'm also envious because I never had that opportunity to learn."
  – *Billie Joe Armstrong* of **Green Day** (1995)

"All you Goths can fuck off back to your tents, The Mission aren't on 'til tomorrow."
  – *Bernard Sumner* of **New Order** (2001)

"The expectations on a woman drive you crazy. If Jennifer Lopez could write songs like Fiona Apple's, she wouldn't have to spend so many hours at the gym."
    – *Shirley Manson* of **Garbage** (2001)

"I think that what Radiohead does, especially in the last two records, sounds fantastic but it feels horrible."
    – *Matthew Good* of **The Matthew Good Band** (2001)

"I make it a point not to talk about my lyrics. I don't feel like being Bono and explaining how high and mighty and smart I am."
    – *Mark Arm* of **Mudhoney** (1995)

"When you start measuring your achievements by records sold and size of gigs you're in trouble. Bananarama sold more records that the Supremes, but are they better?"
    – *Billy Bragg* (1996)

"Elvis didn't write songs. Elvis was a performer. He rocked, but what did he change other than people's hairstyles? Bob Dylan is probably much closer to the soul of rock & roll. Or Gene Vincent maybe."
    – *Paul Westerberg*, ex-**The Replacements**(1993)

"We identify more with people like Victoria Williams, Vic Chesnutt, Will Oldham from Palace, Smog – the meatier songwriters as opposed to a lot of those bands that sound like Son Volt and Uncle Tupelo. Those bands are great too, but there's a lot of watered down versions flooding the record stores."
    – *Joey Burns* of **Calexico** (2001)

"Music is dominated by people way over the hill. There's a sense of generational revolution that we've always been into. People have to decide if we really mean something or if they're going to buy a Rod Stewart Unplugged record. Why these guys are still trying to occupy the limelight, I'll never know."
    – *Ed Roesner* of **Urge Overkill** (1993)

"I think when you get to the point where you don't listen to music anymore, that's when you've gone right up your own arse, isn't it? I think that's a big downfall for a lot of musicians – when you get so involved in your own music you just cut off everything else."
    – *Guy Berryman* of **Coldplay** (2001)

"I once asked John Lennon what he thought of what I do. He said, 'It's great, but it's just rock & roll with lipstick on.'"
    – *David Bowie* (1999)

"If The Beatles were still going today they could've been a bunch of sad old bastards. Everyone going, 'Aw, c'mon Beatles, fucking call it a day man. You've done your bit.'"
    – *Bonehead* of **Oasis** (1995)

"I was very into The Who. But when Who's Next came out, I learned never to trust a band."
    – *Mike Watt* (1995)

"Joe Strummer, he was always the cool one. I didn't like that Mick Jones guy."
    – *Doug Martsch* of **Built To Spill** (1997)

"I don't dislike my peers because they're still around and remind me of what I'm doing. I never liked them anyway."
    –*Robert Smith* of **The Cure** (1993)

"I grew up hating most people. So I became obsessed with movies and television. That's what's real to me, not the world outside my door."
  – **Rob Zombie** (2001)

"I had red, blue, orange, hot pink, and forest green hair in high school. I smoked a lot of pot. I wore used clothing and steel toe boots and terrorized younger wannabe weirdoes. I lit one boy's hair on fire and rubbed tanbark on a girl's head and stuck my finger in her eye. I had a few friends and we hated everyone. I also took French, Spanish, Japanese, and lots of art classes. There were rumors that I was gay, a drug addict, a Satanist, a serial killer, and that my dad was Ozzy Osbourne."
  – *Maya Ford* of **The Donnas** (2001)

"I shot my school principal's daughter with a ball-bearing gun. We didn't get along."
  – *Mark Linkous* of **Sparklehorse** (1998)

"I was just another loser in Portland with a pregnant girlfriend, doing temp jobs, making copies."
  – *Art Alexakis* of **Everclear** (1996)

"What did I do at college? Nothing in particular. They weren't very happy days. In fact, they were really miserable. No, actually, they were the worst days of my life."
  – *J Mascis* of **Dinosaur Jr.** (1993)

"I went form being a cheerleader one year to being a complete freak the next."
  – *Belinda Carlisle* of **The Go-Go's** (2001)

"I was a skinhead years ago. This was before punk and just after mods. I was 15. Then I became a 'suedehead' because I grew my hair some. After that I was a 'casual,' which meant your hair was longer still. Everything was defined by your hair."
  – *Bernard Sumner* of **New Order** (1993)

"When I first got excited about hair was maybe 1984. I brought the Quiet Riot album to the hair salon and said, 'Make me look like Carlos Cavazo.' And they did. And my mom got so upset, she got in the car and drove home without me, which was, like, five miles away.'"
    – *Rivers Cuomo* of **Weezer** (2001)

"When people start talking to you about how you're some spokesperson for a generation, you can't help wondering where the hell that generation was when you were 15."
    – *Adam Duritz* of **The Counting Crows** (1994)

"This whole life that brought me here started out when I was about 13. Hanging around the bowling alleys where people were playing foosball, smoking cigarettes and trying' to get the older guys to buy you some Boone's Farm Strawberry Hill."
    – *Reverend Horton Heat* (1994)

"I was in a bad crowd when I was between 13 and 15; I did more drugs and more wild shit than I did when I was a rock star."
    – *Ed Kowalcyzk* of **Live** (2001)

"I was definitely not a good student in school. I passed because I was, like, kissing my teacher's asses. I never did my homework. I don't know how I made it."
    – *Fred Durst* of **Limp Bizkit** (1999)

"I wanted to drop out of school, but I had a really huge house and my parents both worked, so they were gone a lot of the time. If I quit they probably would have thrown me out of the house, and that would have eliminated any sort of comfort that I had."
    – *Lou Barlow* of **Sebadoh** (1994)

"I'd like to think that a lot of people have a conscience about Napster. Where they use it to find out about music and decide which bands they're going to support and what records they're going to buy.
— *Warren Fitzgerald* of **The Vandals** (2000)

"I think Napster's great. I'm downloading songs from Napster all the time. I don't buy into the bullshit that it's ripping off artists or any of that garbage. I believe it's a great promotional tool. I wish the record industry would look at it that way, but major labels that are supported by the RIAA will never look at it like that because they haven't figured out a way to put a tax or a royalty on it. Because they don't get a cut every time a song is downloaded, they look at it as if they're being robbed. Who says that they have any right to get anything from Napster?"
— *Trever Keith* of **Face To Face** (2000)

"Where does it end? Should journalists work for free? Should lawyers? Engineers? Plumbers? People have been downloading copyrighted music for a couple years now for free, so they think they have the right to do it."
— *Lars Ulrich* of **Metallica** (2000)

"I think Napster is a cool idea, but I agree with it being shut down. What were they thinking? Artists deserve to get paid for their work and record companies are sure as hell going to make sure that they protect their copyrights, and why wouldn't they? I hope they get their shit together and do it right."
— *Marshall Crenshaw* (2000)

"I don't know too much about the MP3 thing, but I hate bootlegging. A lot of times the person playing the stuff wasn't given the option to decide whether they want the stuff heard, or might feel, 'hey, you know what, I had the flu that night, and I don't want anyone to hear that.' You tour as much as we do, you have good nights and bad nights. You don't want people making copies of that, and saying, 'Hey, look at how much Bill sucks.'"
— *Bill Stevenson* of **All** and the **Descendents** (2000)

"The people who are on the board of directors and in the upper-level management of Napster all belong in prison."
— *Howie Klein,* former president of Reprise Records (2000)

"This Limp Bizkit tour is being paid for by Napster. I respect Fred Durst as an artist, but for him to come out with this wholesome, we're-doing-this-for-free act, it's just fake."
— *Lars Ulrich* of **Metallica** (2000)

"People can think whatever they want about me. The fans know the truth. And as for Lars, if that's what he has to say to make himself feel better about his actions, that's fine with me."
— *Fred Durst* of **Limp Bizkit** (2000)

"Is [Durst] saying only kids with computers should get [his music] for free? He should give his music away for free at every retail store in America! The schmuck!"
— *Val Azzoli,* co-CEO of the Atlantic Group (2000)

"The kids who are downloading are being made to look like pirateers. But it happens to be at their fingertips. There needs to be some control."
— *Sheryl Crow* (2000)

"Go on Napster. We recorded nine other songs in addition to the 10 on the record. Go download 'em, it's free."
— *Rivers Cuomo* of **Weezer** (2001)

"Napster is wonderful for a band like mine in its early stages. It's helped us out with curiosity seekers who hear us on the radio, check us out and decide to buy the record."
— *John Ondrasik* of **Five For Fighting** (2001)

"If I'm not talking, then I'm usually eating or smoking."
  – *Michael Stipe* of **R.E.M.** (1995)

"I don't own a gun... I own about 150 guns."
  – *James Hetfield* of **Metallica** (1998)

"I am slowly overcoming the racism that was instilled in me by society."
  – *David Byrne* (1997)

"I like to dress up a lot. Whatever… pirates, cowboys, I think a lot of it is also the way I dress when I go out. I am conscious of the fact that when I put on my Tibetan robes, of which I do have some, and I go out in basically a monk's dress, it stops traffic."
  – *Ian Astbury* of **The Cult** (2001)

"I just sit there on the beach like a lump of wood, really, feeling lonely and sorry for myself. Listening to disco on a cheesy radio."
  – *John Lydon* of **Public Image Ltd.**(1991)

"I want someone to rob a bank in the name of Green Day. I want them to make masks of our faces and rob a fucking bank."
  – *Billie Joe Armstrong* of **Green Day** (1997)

"I had a lot of problems – depression, mood swings, temper tantrums. Someone would get my room service order wrong and I'd smash up the room."
  – *Tricky* (2001)

"I'm not even slightly dangerous to know."
  –*Tom Gray* of **Gomez** (1999)

"I enjoy being a bitch. I enjoy being surrounded by bitches. Boredom is the biggest disease in the world, darling."
  – *Freddie Mercury* of **Queen** (circa 1980)

"I took Spinal Tap real personal. I was really high at the time and Aerosmith was sinking – we were like a boat going down. And that movie was way too close, way too real."
— *Steven Tyler* of **Aerosmith** (1990)

"I've had a gun in my mouth. Just crying and wanting to do it, but not being able to for thought of what it would do to the people I was going to leave behind. It took a hell of a lot more courage to not pull the trigger than it would have taken to pull it."
— *Aaron Lewis* of **Staind** (2001)

"I've been known to fuck a foetus in a slaughterhouse now and again, just to keep things exciting."
— *Marilyn Manson* (1998)

"Being a Beatle was a nightmare."
— *George Harrison* (circa 1987)

"For a while I used the term 'self-defecating' instead of 'self-deprecating.' Finally, someone corrected me."
— *Dave Pirner* of **Soul Asylum** (1993)

"I don't even know my own phone number."
— *Axl Rose* of **Guns N' Roses** (1989)

"I started rapping because I couldn't fucking sing."
— *Coby Dick* of **Papa Roach** (2000)

"I get a clattering in my head when I'm straight that never lets up. I hardly sleep at all."
— *Nick Cave* (1996)

"Drugs, sex with our wives, and masturbation techniques are things we really don't talk about in interviews."
— *Scott Weiland* of **Stone Temple Pilots** (1995)

"It's just whatever – shaving each other's pubes off or waxing each other's chest. Just any excuse to be naughty without having sex. It's just that naughty, tee-hee stuff. We like that kind of behavior."
  – *Courtney Taylor* of **The Dandy Warhols** (2000)

"The only reason we wore sunglasses onstage was because we couldn't stand the sight of the audience."
  – *John Cale* of **The Velvet Underground** (1992)

"I am not the son of Neil Diamond."
  – *Mike D.* of **Beastie Boys** (1994)

"On a bad night I can barely get through "Teen Spirit." I literally want to throw my guitar down and walk away. I can't pretend to have a good time playing it."
  – *Kurt Cobain* of **Nirvana** (1994)

"I'm so uncool, it's unbelievable. I spend my whole life as a geek. It's so unfair."
  – *Shirley Manson* of **Garbage** (1998)

"I'd love it if I went by and heard one of our songs blaring out of a Mexican strip bar."
  – *Peter Buck* of **R.E.M.** (1994)

"I don't ever see [myself getting married]. I want to live a life of depressed freedom."
  – *Morrissey* (1997)

"I fucking hate mayonnaise."
  – *John Curley* of **The Afghan Whigs** (1998)

"On my gravestone, I want it to say, 'I told you I was sick.'"
  – *Tom Waits* (1993)

"Please don't write that we eat, we don't like the fans to think that we eat."
   – *Robin Guthrie* of **Cocteau Twins** (1990)

"Half the time I can't think of anything valid to say, so I just say the most outrageous thing I can."
   – *Noel Gallagher* of **Oasis** (1996)

"I've got a really bad temper. It's very physical. I have that feeling where I want to go off all the time. It's so primal you can't control yourself. And I don't like that. I'll smash the phone up. I mean smash it right to pieces… I'd like to do anger management."
   – *Fran Healy* of **Travis** (2001)

"I'm not a tortured artist, and there's nothing really wrong with me. I just had a bad time for a while."
   – *Elliott Smith* (2001)

"It's funny, I'm still good friends with anyone who's ever been in the band. I'm not a bridge burner and I don't talk shit about people after they leave. I don't have any enemies. We're all still good buddies. I'm even still good buddies with Greg [Ginn] and Henry [Rollins] and everybody."
   – *Bill Stevenson* of **All** and the **Descendents**,
      ex-**Black Flag** (2000)

"A long time ago, I used to get drunk and hang out a lot at mental institutions. The girls there are all loose and they are…fun, you know?"
   – *Joey Ramone* (circa 1980)

"I actually contemplate suicide every day. My record sales would certainly go up."
   – *J. Mascis* of **Dinosaur Jr.** (1994)

"If you want to torture me, you'd tie me down and force me to watch our first five videos."
    – **Jon Bon Jovi** of **Bon Jovi** (2000)

"I have a lot of responsibilities so I'm not about to spend the night in a Danish bar in the go-go cage with some cheap... actually, no, let's go."
    – *E* of the **Eels** (1998)

"It's actually come as quite a shock to learn just how many people don't like me."
    – *Phil Collins* (circa 1990)

"I'm obviously not Eddie Van Halen, but I know my four chords."
    – *Mark Lanegan,* ex-**Screaming Trees**(1998)

"I like to go to the graveyard, lay down on somebody's grave, take a bottle out there, dance around naked, y'know?"
    –*Tom Waits* (1983)

"My reputation as a tyrant, Svengali, asshole, there's truth in that."
    – *Billy Corgan* of **Smashing Pumpkins** (1994)

"I'm not that interested in the rest of the world. My interests don't go much beyond the four walls of my apartment."
    – *Mark Kozelek* of **Red House Painters** (1995)

"I don't feel like I'm beautiful a lot of the time. I don't feel like I'm ugly, but I did spend a lot of my time having people tell me I'm ugly."
    – *Fiona Apple* (1997)

"One of the things that freaked out Krist and Kurt and I when Nirvana became popular was that people were looking at us like we were supposed to be role models. The thought of anyone looking up to me frightens me, because what does anyone see in me that they don't have within themselves?"
    – *Dave Grohl* of **The Foo Fighters** (2001)

"I don't think what I do is original at all. It's more out of faithfulness to my adolescent dreams that I'm still doing this."
– *Rivers Cuomo* of **Weezer** (2000)

"Pieces Of You" is not a good record. It's an embarrassing record, ultimately."
– *Jewel* (1998)

"I have incredibly long spells of catatonia after I finish a record. And weird visions that are not pleasant. Sitting there, being wide-awake, imagining yourself falling out of an airplane."
– *Bob Mould*, of **Sugar**, ex-**Husker Du** (1996)

"I try not to be a hypocrite, though I don't think there's any doubt that I can make a total prat of myself."
– *Billy Bragg* (1993)

"People sometimes ask me if I'm happy, and I tell them to fuck off."
– *Thom Yorke* of **Radiohead** (1995)

"I get a wild energy when I hang out with junkies."
– *Tim Armstrong* of **Rancid** (1995)

"Although I may have a head full of anger, I don't think it'd be very easy to kill someone unless I had a large shotgun or a can of gasoline and a match. I would love to fire a gun, I've often though that."
– *PJ Harvey* (2000)

"I always wanted to be able to speak and express myself in a way that wasn't full of fear and inhibition."
– *Peter Murphy*, ex-**Bauhaus** (1995)

"I listen to The Germs on the beach because it gets everyone upset and makes them move away so I can have more of the beach to myself."
– *Flea* of the **Red Hot Chili Peppers** (1995)

"I love it when somebody insults me. That means that I don't have to be nice anymore."
  – *Billy Idol* (1990)

"'The Boss' was an idiotic nickname. It's the bane of my entire career. I've learned to live with it but I've hated it y'know."
  – *Bruce Springsteen* (1996)

"I like doing stuff in the produce aisles, you know – putting my fingers in bananas or whatever. I like eating chocolates and the stuff that's out there in the bins. In terms of, like, reckless behavior, like getting drunk and driving a car ninety miles an hour off a cliff type behavior, I've done all that. It's fine at the time, maybe once or twice, but it's dangerous."
  – *Ian Astbury* of **The Cult** (2001)

"I can fart twenty-one times."
  – *Mark Hoppus* of **Blink 182** (2000)

"If I ever take me own life, Noel's coming too. The split second before, I'm killing him."
  – *Liam Gallagher* of **Oasis** (1995)

"I never liked the Beatles."
  –*Trent Reznor* of **Nine Inch Nails** (1997)

"I've always quit everything I wanted to. I quit school, I quit hundreds of jobs, I quit girlfriends, I quit bands. This band is the only thing I've ever stuck with, and I've never wanted to quit anything so badly. Every other day I'm, like, 'Okay, that is it.'"
  – *Ben Folds* of the **Ben Folds Five** (1999)

"People think I'm a bitch, but I'm really just shy."
  – *Kat Bjelland* of **Babes in Toyland** (1995)

"Some people really love rim jobs, I don't."
  – *Kurt Heasley* of **The Lilys** (1999)

"I've sinned so many ways it's unbelievable. I've robbed stores. I've had plenty of sex. I've lied terribly. I've cheated. I've been greedy. I've lusted. I've done it all."
  – *Fred Durst* of **Limp Bizkit** (1999)

"I wish I was in the Basketball Hall of Fame, but that's not gonna happen."
  – *Ad-Rock* of **Beastie Boys** (2000)

"I can make a much better record, I underachieve, really."
  – *David Gray* (2001)

"Taking me seriously is a big mistake. I certainly wouldn't."
  – *Fiona Apple* (1999)

"You think I'm an asshole now, you should've seen me when I was drunk."
  – *John Mellencamp* (circa 1992)

"I truthfully do enjoy pornography. I think it's funny, ridiculous, absurd, disgusting, and entertaining."
  – *Tad Doyle* of **Tad** (1994)

"I don't want to be anyone's revolutionary. I don't want to lead a movement. I mean, it turns me off so much."
  – *Liz Phair* (1994)

"I have a certain way with words when it comes to violence. I just enjoy ruminating over the details."
  – *Nick Cave* (1996)

"I pushed myself to the point of becoming this caricature of a rock star that was so good he was in danger of killing himself."
  – *Dave Gahan* of **Depeche Mode** (1995)

"If I'm crazy enough to think it, then I'm crazy enough to say it. That's how I base my whole shit."
  – *Eminem* (1999)

"My father would make me stand up straight and sing the national anthem four times. Then we'd sit down and eat air meals to practice handling silverware or practice 'seating the lady.' I have impeccable table manners."
   – *Henry Rollins* (circa 1993)

"My mum has got really good taste. She would be a brilliant A&R person."
   – *Fran Healy* of **Travis** (2001)

"My parents were Baptists...Really hardcore religious people...I guess that's why I'm so pissed off."
   –*Todd Lewis* of **The Toadies** (1996)

"I remember one time I asked my pop what religion we were. He said, 'capitalist.'"
   – *Mike Diamond* of **Beastie Boys** (1994)

"The fighting did stem from being brothers and songwriting partners. We sat around with guitars and were writing songs together. That's not easy. Being siblings is not easy. Being fellow songwriters is not easy, but being both is really a bit much."
   – *Chris Robinson* of **The Black Crowes** on
      bandmate/brother Rich (2001)

"There are all of these expectations that come with this 'Sixties offspring' bullshit but I can't tell you how little [my father] had to do with my music. I met him one time when I was eight; other than that, there was nothing."
   – *Jeff Buckley* (1994)

"The thing about nursing is that you do have enforced thinking time for hours and hours and hours a day. Having a daughter has made me put my ear to the ground and hear what people are saying."
   – *Tori Amos* (2001)

"Becoming a father was a real watershed, and it's out of my job perspective. I don't keel over if I don't get on "Top Of The Pops" or the cover of NME or the top of the bill anymore."
  – *Billy Bragg* (1996)

"I'm waiting for my kids to grow up and get into the Offspring and look at me like I'm a total candy-ass."
  – *Jakob Dylan* of **The Wallflowers** (2000)

"To be called an elder statesman is so unbelievably insulting. Brad Pitt is exactly three years younger than me."
  – *Michael Stipe* of **R.E.M.** (2001)

"We never bought into that Pete Townshend 'Hope I die before I get old' crap. We love our beer bellies, and you're gonna too."
  – *Johnny Rotten,* on the reformation of
  The Sex Pistols (1996)

"I guess I don't so much mind being old, as I mind being fat and old."
  – *Peter Gabriel* (1992)

"I know I've reached the age where other artists would bleach their hair or buy a fancy costume, but I'm not inclined towards either presenting a new persona or even presenting myself as the person Smiths apostles felt they knew more intimately than their own friends."
  – *Morrissey* (1991)

"I'm not going bald, my head's just getting higher."
  – *Angus Young* of **AC/DC** (1992)

"I don't want to be an oldies act. Then where do you end up? Las Vegas… the elephants' graveyard of rock stars."
  – *Billy Joel* (2001)

"I don't think I'll be interested in making records when I get to Bowie's age."
  – *Lloyd Cole* (1984)

"I don't want to try to be 25. I was 25, and I had a great time. I want my music and my performance to reflect who I am at the time and not try to chase something. I had my moment of being the new, hip thing."
  – *Melissa Etheridge* (1997)

"What we're doing for this tour is stocking up on Geritol and Viagra; we've got some Formula 44 and the Helsinki treatment. Our vehicle is like an oxygen tank on wheels. I need a walker and an electric chair."
  — *Keith Morris* gears up for **The Circle Jerks**
    reunion tour (2001)

"I'm just glad to be feeling better. I really thought I'd be seeing Elvis soon."
  — *Bob Dylan* survives a life-threating illness (1997)

"I'm like a car. I'm like a really well kept classic car. You might be driving along the road in it — it's got a great paint job, everybody's checking you out, girls are going, 'Whoa! Love your car! — And then you go blowing a piston through the hood. It's like, 'Oh, fuck. Gotta call AAA.'"
  — *Iggy Pop* (2001)

"In 1974, I wrote a poem called 'Ten Thousand Iggys.' Like someday, there'll be 10,000 of me running around. Now there are millions. They're mine whether they know it or not! Because with me, it was never really a look, it was my behavior that caught on."
  —*Iggy Pop* (1995)

"Before I had my own band, Blue Oyster Cult had heard me reading poetry and thought of having me involved in the band, but I had never sung it and it had never occurred to me to be in a rock and roll band."
  — *Patti Smith* (2000)

"My first gigs were on L.A. buses. I'd sing about Axl Rose, the levee, bus passes and strychnine."
  — *Beck* (1994)

"In England I worked as a postal worker at night in between college. One night I was singing to myself "Don't Be Cruel" by Elvis Presley or a Lou Reed song, "Vicious" or something, and a bloke said the classic, 'Don't ever try singing for a living.' Eleven albums and a career spanning the world and I can still hear him saying it to me."
  — *Billy Idol* (circa 1991)

"There's this English fantasy about going to London with just your hat in your hand and making your fortune. We all did that. We all wanted to be in a band. We lived in the same building – this massive place where 500 people lived. And there were about 100 people with guitars. We were lucky to have each other. Because on my own, I'm shit."
  —*Chris Martin* of **Coldplay** (2001)

"We were just hanging around, you know, getting stoned and watching TV at Steve's parents house, and we'd started making up these songs. Steve had just started being a DJ at UVA and I think he just got the idea that, well, there's all these bands, we can do it too. It was a completely naïve thing."
  — *Scott Kannenberg* of **Pavement** (1994)

"Everyone gave us advice. Every day of the goddamn week. 'Get some hot chicks in bikinis! Get some disco drums!' You go, 'Really? On Murmur?' Disco drums! It's obvious that these people didn't listen to the records. It's great – people who have never, ever signed a band that has been successful will tell you how to make your band a success."
— *Peter Buck* of **R.E.M.** (1991)

"The first thing I sang with the band was Bryan Adams' "Summer of '69.""
— *Ed Kowalczyk* of **Live** (1994)

"We were inspiring each other. I miss (the 1960s) quite a bit. I think about how great music was then and how inspired everybody was. It seems like it's all gone away. People aren't making very many records these days."
— *Brian Wilson* of **The Beach Boys** (2001)

"I'm glad we started out at ground zero and went gradually to where we are instead of having it happen overnight. We probably would've turned into assholes and written shitty songs."
— *Jason Black* of **Hot Water Music** (2001)

"When we started it was very underground. We had to struggle and scamper just to play anywhere we could play and open the doors for all these other bands."
— *Keith Morris* of **The Circle Jerks** (2000)

"I played the piano in church. I even taught bible school one year. Then I got into the greatest gospel hits of the '70s, and it was all over."
— *Axl Rose* of **Guns and Roses** (1989)

"In the early 70's, I really wanted to be in a band and I actually tried to take guitar lessons from this guy who lived on my street. He didn't really know how to play guitar. It was a scam, although he did teach me to play, not the chords, but the notes to "Smoke On The Water." I

only had that one guitar lesson. Then we tried to form bands. We had a band and basically we'd go out and shoplift toy guitars and smash them, because we'd just seen Woodstock and we just thought that was the coolest."
  — *Ian MacKaye* of **Fugazi** (1996)

"Every incarnation of the Soft Boys was based around heavily rehearsing. We were the antithesis of, say, the Rolling Stones or something, who write their records in the studio. Everything was always rehearsed someplace near a café where you could buy egg and chips."
  — *Robyn Hitchcock* (2001)

"Kid Rock always had this vision, and I tagged along like a younger brother. When I first met him, he was wearing the hat flipped up and the clock around his neck. I was thirteen, he was probably sixteen. I looked up to him. I still do."
  — *Uncle Kracker* (2001)

"I remember Aaron coming to my house for the first time and singing. I said, 'Where have you been for fifteen years? I've been looking for you!'"
  — *Mike Mushock* of **Staind** (2001)

"When [The Replacements] made our first record, the producer wasn't smiling at all. He slapped the Ramones record on, A/B'd them, played them at the same time and said, 'Well, it's louder than theirs!' That was his only comment."
  — *Paul Westerberg,* ex-**The Replacements** (1989)

"In the old days, when we toured, you always brought the newer band with you to open up. I brought Screaming Trees, Black Flag brought The Minutemen, Sonic Youth brought Firehose on their first tour."
  — *Mike Watt,* ex-**Minutemen** and **fIREHOSE** (1995)

"The minute we started rehearsing and Ed started singing – which was within an hour of him landing in Seattle – was the first time I was like, 'Wow, this is a band that I'd play at home on my stereo.'"
  – *Jeff Ament* of **Pearl Jam** (2001)

"If I listen now to our first record, there are things that I wish I hadn't said, or thought about before saying them. But I'm glad for the opportunity to have made mistakes and learn from those mistakes."
  – *Ad-Rock* of **Beastie Boys** (2000)

"When we first started out, success was the farthest thing from our minds. We'd just, like, you know, get together and smoke pot and play in circles for hours. Laugh, joke and have fun. People started coming to the shows and it turned into something."
  – *Roddy Bottum* of **Faith No More** (1995)

"When we started, the fashionable thing was for a pop group to consist of one chap with a peculiar haircut and a synthesizer, and another chap warbling while doing exotic dancing. We were about as far away from that as you could get."
  – *Jem Finer* of **The Pogues** (1993)

"I was just so fed up with this amplifier that I had, it just wouldn't make the sound that I wanted it to. So out of frustration I got out a razor blade and I cut the cone up. I didn't even think for a minute that it was going to work, and then I plugged it in and it made that amazing distorted sound. I really did feel that something new had happened. Both Ray and I knew we were on to something. I should have patented it, I'd be really well off."
  – *Dave Davies* of **The Kinks,** uncredited inventor of distortion (2000)

"Black Flag was a lot of hungry times, a lot of missed meals, sleeping in your wet clothes in the back of the van. Imagine living in Das Boot for five years."
  – *Henry Rollins*, ex-**Black Flag** (1994)

"We heard the first tower go down. Smoke wrapped around from either side of the window, as if it were arms wrapping around our window, and the view disappeared. That was the moment everything stopped being normal. We ran out the door…down fifteen flights to the lobby, and it was full of smoke. There were bloody people pouring into it."
   – Rhett Miller of **Old 97's**

"Everyone I know in New York is sobbing. "Who has done this? How can anyone ever justify taking a single life? The world is going to be different now."
   – Moby

"The streets are empty downtown except for the few who live there, trancelike, going about their day to day lives, walking their dogs, going to work, or just walking. At some ghostly unseen signal everyone turns his or her heads, cranes their necks, looking to the patch of sky where, twenty-four hours ago, the mountainous peaks of those two towers stood."
   – David Bowie

"Normal life stuff, including the very act of being in a touring rock band, seems incredibly strange. Everyone feels terrible for the victims of this, and a sense of frustrating anger over an inability to do anything about it."
   – A statement from the members of **Weezer**

"I think that each and every one of us should look inside our own hearts and examine our own personal acts of terrorism, hatred, intolerance, negativity, the list goes on and on. We're all responsible. It's not just Bin Laden, it's all of us, we've all contributed to hatred in the world today."
   – Madonna

"On [the day of the attack] the victims were American. But the horrible scenes that we've witnessed on TV this week are regular occurrences in other places around the globe. And too often, violence like this has been meted out by our own country and its client states. We should stand together against this type of violence in all its forms, whenever it happens, whether it's done in the name of religious fanaticism, or in the name of our own domestic elite."

   – Tom Morello of **Rage Against The Machine**

"Would I be angry if a relative of mine was killed and would I hold a grudge forever? It would be very hard not to."

   – Perry Farrell of **Jane's Addiction**

"I'm so disappointed when I hear people starting to divide America up into who is American and who isn't."

   – Dave Matthews

"Whether you're a country being invaded or a person being invaded, your trust goes, you're vulnerable, and you ask yourself, 'What does freedom mean?'"

   – Tori Amos

"When it happened, it made me think, 'Fuck you!' Fuck anyone that's going to bomb the city where my kids live because of a political difference. My kids are half American. My wife was American, born in New York. I have a lot of family here. But, most important, it's about what America stands for. Love it or hate it, it stands for freedom. And I get very emotional about that."

   – Paul McCartney

"I'm not leaving New York. And neither is anyone else. We're here. We are quintessential Americans – we're not only American but New York-American."

   – Lou Reed

"Life is what happens to you while you're busy making other plans."
  – *John Lennon* (1980)

"Smoking cigarettes isn't enough. There's no way around pain. That's part of the chain of being alive."
  – *Alanis Morrissette* (1995)

"It's astonishing how dark your life can get without you even noticing. It slips and slips further away. You think it's just stress, so you push on. And that gets you into even worse situations and you slide further."
  – *Tricky* (2001)

"I still spend a lot of time thinking about what a 15-year-old must be thinking right now, because that is the predominant audience that you're going to be relating to. And there are still a lot of issues from that time of my life that are unresolved."
  – *Billy Corgan* of **Smashing Pumpkins** (1996)

"I've definitely developed this karmic approach to everything I do now. When something bad happens, you just have to get your head down and soldier on, for the benefit of your own peace of mind. I believe if you continue to follow your instincts and what you believe in, then things will somehow work out."
  – *Tim Burgess* of **The Charlatans U.K.** (2000)

"We don't stuff our personal demons inside us, we get them out. It's therapeutic."
  – *Layne Staley* of **Alice In Chains** (1994)

"They way I feel inside is, 'Come with me, I'd love to have you.' That's true of every facet of my life. That's the option I'm giving to everybody. I haven't said it to anyone, but that's the way I'm feeling. In reference to people who listen to us, in reference to everything. Like, 'I'm going this way, and anybody who wants to come is absolutely welcome. But I'm going there, with or without you.'"
  – *Dave Matthews* (2001)

"Reality is not about being cool. There are other things in life to deal with. You can't entertain a baby with cynicism."
   – *Kim Gordon* of **Sonic Youth** (1996)

"I'm not afraid a lot, just disappointed. I guess, the more I experience, the more I take comfort in knowing that everyone follows the same trends in life. You know, birth, maturity, some sort of mid-life crises – well, before that, I guess you find something to do, a career."
   – *Greg Graffin* of **Bad Religion** (1996)

"Practically everyone is going through an identity crisis. The whole fucking planet's trying to figure out who they are and why they're here. And so are we."
   – *Mike D.* of **Beastie Boys** (2000)

"I worked in a funeral home in college and I saw people brought in body bags. They'd lay them out on the tile table and put a little rubber wedge beneath their head. I always thought they should take you in there when you're twenty and have that I-don't-care-if-I-die James Dean syndrome."
   – *Chris Isaak* (1995)

"I'm much more concerned with what it means to be a good person, and what it means to have a fulfilling life. Those are the things I'm thinking about and writing about. But I still have the same hopes and fears that I had before, and still feel kind of vulnerable to life."
   – *Stephan Jenkins* of **Third Eye Blind** (1998)

"I was one of those people who had a hard time adapting to life after college… I had problems with getting into bad situations and avoiding getting out of them. I've really changed that around, and things are a lot better now."
   – *Mary Timony* of **Helium** (1995)

"I like to treat every opportunity in life as just that, as an opportunity. You meet people and you talk. I think in explaining yourself you get to understand what you're doing a little more."
  – *Sting* (2000)

"Depression can be very inspiring. At least for me it can be. The quiet aspects of life are very important, because let's face it, life is pretty difficult."
  – *Chris Cornell,* ex-**Soundgarden** (1999)

"I don't want to live in an ivory tower, being the songwriter who just turns inward. I always want to be a part of the whole thing. That's why I live a pretty normal life at home, go shopping, all that. It's part of my life, and I don't want to have that part of my life taken from me."
  – *Billie Joe Armstrong* of **Green Day** (2000)

"There are two rules to living well. The first is, don't sweat the little shit. The second is, it's all little shit. In other words, it's all okay. We may be lost, but we're way ahead of schedule. So... let's dance!"
  – *David Lee Roth* (1986)

"How can you find yourself if you don't lose yourself? How can you be renewed if you don't get old? There have to be peaks and valleys, or it's boring."
  – *Neil Young* (circa 1997)

"I don't have any agenda for the human race except maybe, 'don't fuck with me and I won't fuck with you.'"
  – *Mark Arm* of **Mudhoney** (1995)

"My theory is that when people die, they spend their first few days in heaven laughing their asses off for being so stupid while they were alive. Just finally getting the joke."
  – *Joan Osborne* (1995)

Tim Armstrong of **Rancid**

Photo by Rahav Segev/Photopass.com

Access
Addicted To Noise
Alternative Press
Aquarian Weekly
Austin Chronicle
Babe Hound
Bad Monkey
Beats
Big Takeover
Billboard
CDNow
Chicago Tribune
CMJ
Creative Loafing
Creem
Dallas Observer
Details
Entertainment Weekly
Forced Exposure
Gear
Guitar Player
Guitar World
Hot Press
Huh
Interview
Ill Literature
Irish Times
Jam! Showbiz
Kerrang
Lime Lizard
Loaded
Los Angeles Times
Melody Maker
Magnet
Metro Active

Modern Rock Live
Mojo
Ms.
MTV
Musician
Muse
Music.com
New Musical Express
New Route
New York
NY Rock
The Onion
Option
Penthouse
People
Philadelphia City Paper
Playboy
Q
Raygun
Record Collector
Reflex
Request
Rockpile
Rockpool
Rolling Stone
San Jose Mercury News
Select
Sonicnet
Spin
Static
Starline
The Stranger
Us
Vox

I'd like to thank my beautiful wife Heidi for the inspiration and encouragement, and for giving me two of the loveliest daughters a father could ask for in Meredith and Hayley.

Big love to my parents, Dave & Pinky Luerssen and my mother-in-law, Marie Garner. Further family hugs and high fives: Liz & Ron Peed, Ann, John, Jane & Theo Crowther, David & Caitlin Everett, Marianne Mercer, George Mercer, Dick, Harriet and Jay Mercer, James Luerssen, Jennifer Luerssen, The Edmondson's, Sherry Solomon, The Yingling's, The Millilli's, The Frederick's. Additionally, the memories of Cmdr. James W. Mercer, Emily S. Luerssen and Ralph W. Garner cannot go unnoticed.

Monster thanks to Angelo Deodato, Bill & Kerrianne Cort, Mike & Je McGonigal, The Jardim's, John Kieltyka, The Murins, Dan Yemin, Andy Rockman, Ben Forgash, Bill Boyle, Bill Beedenbender, Todd Pearsall, Jason Karian, Chrissy Diaz, Doug Heintz and Jeff Heintz for your friendship over the years.

Extra thanks to Jim "I'll drive, I'll buy" Walsh, Mike "The Keymaster" Keith, Gary "Lodge" Hoffman, "Fearless" Noel Christmas, Nick Catania, Bob Kelly, Jimmy Kulpa, Ian Duthie, Brian Morris, The Luka's and the rest of my PSE&G co-workers for your daily laughs and enlightenment.

Special props to Bill Crandall at Rolling Stone for your guidance and friendship, you've helped/mentored me in countless ways. Nods for past and present editorial support go to Jonathan Cohen, Andrew Dansby, David Sprague, Mike McKee, Tom Pryor, Peter Gaston, Drew Wheeler, Allison Stewart, Joe D'Angelo, Shirley Halperin, Jennifer Vineyard, Brian W. Parks, Andy Gensler, Jim Dolan, and Shirronda Sweet.

Further thanks to a number of musicians, writers and music industry folks for help and general inspiration, including Jim DeRogatis, Hilary Okun, Jason Loewenstein, Derek Meier, Heidi Anne-Noel, Strummer/ Jones, Legs McNeil, Mickey Melchiondo, Chris Jacobs, Robert Pollard,

Andy Partridge, Jason Consoli, Andy Adelewitz, Tommy Keene, Josh Bloom, Elvis Costello, Paul Westerberg., Rahav Segev, Jason Homa, Dominic Episcopo, Mike Doughty, Britt Daniel, Pat Wilson , John Flansburgh, Steve Kingston, Howard Stern, and Gary Stewart.

I'd especially like to thank Alexandra Zorn, Joanne Abrams, Dan Shepelavy, Jerod Gunsberg, and Stanley Hartman at The Telegraph Company. Glad to be on board.

Sorry if I forgot anyone.

About the Author

John D. Luerssen is a regular news, reviews and features contributor to *Rolling Stone, Billboard* and CDNow. He has also written for *VH1.com, Music.com, Musicblitz, Pop Culture Press, Rockpile, Bop* and *Smug Magazine*.

He lives in Westfield, New Jersey with his wife and two daughters.

Comments and feedback are always welcome. Please write to John at *rockquotebook@hotmail.com*.

For further information about the photographs in this book, please visit: Rahav Segev–*www.photopass.com,* Jason Homa–*www.jasonhomaphotography.com,* Dominic Episcopo–*www.episcopo.com*